He's Much Better,
He Can Smile Now

He's Much Better, He Can Smile Now

Children Learn to Live

Tom Wakefield

DAVID & CHARLES
Newton Abbot   London   Vancouver

0 7153 6707 2

© Tom Wakefield 1974

Set in 11 on 13pt Pilgrim and printed in
Great Britain by John Sherratt & Son Ltd.,
Altrincham, Cheshire WA14 5QQ
for David & Charles (Holdings) Limited,
South Devon House, Newton Abbot, Devon.

Published in Canada by Douglas David &
Charles Limited, 3645 McKechnie Drive,
West Vancouver BC.

CONTENTS

ACKNOWLEDGEMENTS

My thanks are due to parents, friends and colleagues who have helped in the preparation of this book. The teachers named are not camouflaged by pseudonyms. On the other hand, the children and parents could be found in any urban educational priority area anywhere. To all of them, wherever they may be, I am grateful.

For Doreen, Rosie and Robert

Once upon a time, in a very lonely place lived a man endowed by nature with extraordinary curiosity and a very penetrating mind. For a pastime he raised birds, whose songs he much enjoyed, and he observed with great admiration the happy contrivances by which they could transform at will the very air they breathed into a variety of sweet songs.

One night this man chanced to hear a delicate song close to his house and being unable to connect it with anything but some small bird he set out to capture it. When he arrived at a road he found a shepherd boy who was blowing into a kind of hollow stick while moving his fingers about on the wood, thus drawing from it a variety of notes similar to those of a bird, though by quite a different method. Puzzled, but impelled by his natural curiosity he gave the boy a calf in exchange for his flute and returned to solitude. But realising that if he had not chanced to meet the boy he would never have learned of the existence of a new method of forming musical notes and the sweetest songs, he decided to travel to distant places in the hope of meeting with some new adventure.

'The Assayer' – Galileo

1

A DROP OF BLOOD

'Sorry, I late. I mean I couldn't come to the parents' meeting last week – you can see, can't you. I just came to see if Rufus was any better. It's so hard at home right now.'

'Come in, Mrs St Stephen. When is the baby due – soon? Sit down love. Rosemary, could I have a cup of tea for Mrs St Stephen?'

'Tom, telephone.'

'Hallo – no, I can't let you have those figures today. I am with a mother, yes, a mother. Help yourself to sugar.'

By this time Mrs St Stephen has lowered herself into the chair. She is thirty-four, attractive, very pregnant and very tired. Rufus, up to this moment, has been with us for two and a half years. He entered school as an 'emergency' admission. A beautiful child with large brown eyes and a face that only changed expression according to the intensity of its frown. It almost seemed impossible that a six-year-old could achieve such facial limitations. There were no answers or interests registered to toys, rocking horse or pictures or sweets, and physical efforts of comfort were rejected like the shock from an electric kettle. I asked Mrs St Stephen if she wished to stay with him on the first day, but there were younger children at home, washing to be collected, payments to be made . . .

Brenda Harding was in charge of the reception class at the

time – teaching background infants and primary, plus experience in day maladjusted schools. She had recently married and was deeply in love and most happy. At twenty-five she was serene, organised and lovingly competent with her children. A deep voice, a very deep voice for a child, said, 'Keep my coat on.' Brenda didn't argue with Rufus.

'Lawrence, are you going to look after Rufus today?'

'And me, Mrs Harding, and me, and me . . .'

'Yes, Patsy, and Leroy, what a lot of friends he's going to have . . .'

Brenda smiled her 'I don't need you any more' smile and I left quietly.

Within the first month Rufus had established his first means of communication. It was quite simple. He attacked physically any children who came within his range. In many instances of aggression amongst children, it is the provocative children who are hurt. Consequently, one must be fair to both the injurers and the injured. However, no children seemed beyond Rufus's lethal orbit. The kicks and the slaps were delivered swiftly during play-time – followed by screams, crying, sobs, then comfort and condolence from concerned children and adults.

We tried to form or create other areas for Rufus's self-esteem – let him go first for his meal – never asked him to share his sweets. All his paintings were for him, group paintings in which he had participated – just for him. In play, either recreational or educational, he could not compete, share, or parallel any skill, activity or achievement. Praise is so much a part of our working day that we are often surprised when visitors to the school express astonishment at the extent of its variety and delivery. Brenda Harding had begun to praise Rufus through other children and slowly the chrysalis began to change its shape. In the third month, as I was talking to Brenda in the classroom, she indicated that D-Day was at hand. I admired some work the children had completed – a group effort – and was on the point of leaving.

'Mr Wakefield, did you see Rufus's lorry?' said Brenda over her shoulder. She was tying Trudy's shoe-lace. Sybil Thorndike couldn't have timed it better.

'It's there, on the shelf.'

I looked at the shell of a toilet roll and the four cotton reels with a small half-potato on top.

'That's the best lorry I've seen in Hackney. I wish I had one.' I meant it.

When the school opened I was equipped with a nasty buzzing machine with three buttons. I pressed the red one and a light lit up outside the door saying 'Come In'. The green said 'Wait Please' and the yellow one said 'Engaged'. I hated it. It made my room a cross between a robot's sanctuary and a public lavatory. Somehow it got broken after a few days and since then I have left the door open when parents or visitors are not with me. Even then, none of my children are afraid to knock. I see no reason why doctors, inspectors and administrative officers should not have every opportunity of seeing and hearing the children they are partly responsible for. If particularly private conversations are necessary, then Rosemary, my secretary, carries on in my absence.

'Oh, I'll tell Mr Wakefield, Sharon, I know he'll be pleased . . .'

It was during one such private time that a tremendous thump was delivered on the door. Before Rosemary could get round to the entrance, my door was flung open. The Administrative Officer looked slightly alarmed. Rufus marched in, knocking the rocking horse to one side.

'Lorry, for you.'

'For me?'

'Yes.'

'Can I show Mrs Perraudin?'

'Yes.'

'Rufus, I'm so glad. I'm putting the lorry on my desk and I shall look at it all day. Would you like some Smarties?'

'Yes. A red, a yellow – not a brown one.'

'Here's a yellow one, and a red one for you – and would you like to give Mrs Harding the brown one?'

'No, it's for Julie.'

'Oh, all right. Is she your friend?'

There was no answer. I'm sure the Administrative Officer hadn't a clue as to why I was smiling. No, the ventilation was not good enough (Rufus had begun to share). Yes, I did realise that he was in control of placement (Rufus had begun to share). I did realise the cost of an individual guide – but Victor was at risk (Rufus had begun to share) and needed one. Always in this work I know what should be done. I am exhausted each term by what can't be done. The Administrative Officer was placing his trilby on his head and Rufus St Stephen was sharing a brown Smartie with Julie Franklin.

As Mrs St Stephen sipped her tea, fragments of biscuit fell on to the saucer. She asked after Mrs Harding.

'She's in Worcester now – having her own baby soon.'

'Oh, I'm glad for her – she want a baby?'

'Yes.'

I waited, knowing that Mrs St Stephen wanted to talk about herself.

'You not angry with me about changing my mind about sending Rufus to a boarding school?'

'No, I'm pleased. I think you do very well.'

'I try, but Rufus is a great trouble – the people in the flats are no help. Always complaining about him – he is better at home now. He don't hit the little children quite so much and he talks more.' There is a long pause. 'Mr Wakefield, I'm afraid for the new baby. If it a boy, not too bad – but Rufus say if it a girl . . . could you talk to him?'

'We will visit you in Hackney Hospital. Mrs Munson will bring Rufus. I'm sure it will be fine.'

'Thank you, yes he's much better, he holds my hand now. He would never let me cuddle him as a child, you know – not like the others at all.'

Mrs St Stephen rose slowly, preparing to leave – yet I felt, as with so many harassed mothers, she would have preferred to forego the pressures of family life and home and to have stayed with us if she could. I thought of the two rooms and the kitchen, the four children and wondered if the new bed would be a bunk-bed or a fold-up.

Mrs St Stephen turned as I reached for the door handle.

'I didn't have a bad time with Rufus you know – he born easily.' She shook her head. 'There's no 'counting for his problems. Only one thing I can think – it may not be nothing though.'

I waited.

'You know my situation; well, when Rufus was two I had to go out to work and this lady – a near neighbour, she look after him. I pay her. Rufus with her all day and she say he never cry. He was with her two and a half years. But once I remember I see blood in the pram and it upset me then. Still it's all past now.'

She leaves with a warm smile and my admiration, waving to me as she waddles past my window.

I went in to see Lis Munson (Rufus's new teacher) and peered through the glass door. Rufus was working on a huge collage connected with the circus. There were five children working on it. Paints, crayons, milk bottle tops were being transformed into a crazy clown. Rufus was doing quite a bit of bossing and pushing but he was sharing – what's more, three of the five children were girls.

'Lis, sorry, I'm a bit late – will send the assembly note round in five minutes. Any birthdays?'

'Yes, Robin.'

'And me, and me,' says Rufus.

'No, it's not your birthday. But look at this Mr Wakefield – Rufus's batman story – shall we give Rufus a clap?'

'I want everybody clap,' boomed Rufus.

He meant all the school. We all did applaud him in

assembly. His slow smile still remains enigmatic. He will hold our hands. He can sing. He can draw. He can count and is beginning to read. Yet, I wonder, with all the nurture we can offer, will those two and a half 'pram-years' with the spot of blood – real or imaginary – indelibly imprinted on his mother's mind and mine, ever be eradicated?

Circumstances, conditions and social backgrounds have to be accountable for so much. Islamic parents might accept it all as fate – as pre-ordained. In some ways this is very much like the attitude behind the fatigued Stanford Binet intelligence tests which help to determine whether or not a child is educationally sub-normal. Admittedly, they are only a part of a referral process – there are reports from doctors, head teachers, teachers and sometimes psychologists. There is no doubt that all the children on arrival in school are very backward, but it is also clear that many of them are emotionally disturbed, deeply depressed and in many instances, most desperately unhappy. What seems to have been discounted are their feelings, which have been bludgeoned and battered to such an extent that intellectual effort seems worthless. If these feelings are nursed, even partially, then the IQs (which are supposed to be reasonably constant) seem to grow more quickly than a runner bean.

At least half of the school intake could come into this category if it were possible to make our nurture and care any more intensive, but as it is, when I look at the staff after each term, I am reminded of an egg blown clear of the yolk. It has been always clear to me that caring in any form is a wearing process; care must be felt and feelings need to be organised to be productive.

The building is officially recognised by the DES as a school for educationally sub-normal children. In terms of the wording of the 1944 Act, there is no doubt that all the children here are correctly placed: 'Pupils who by reasons of limited ability or other conditions resulting in educational retardation require some other specialised form of education wholly or partly in substitution for the education given in ordinary schools.'

'Other conditions' blankets a great deal of ground and one questions the applicability of the phrase sub-normal to any child. Educationally handicapped might pass – but sub-normal? In spite of 'other conditions', these children often manage much more than a mere social survival. Most adults working with them express astonishment at their resilience to social and emotional pressures that would cause the collapse of an older person and are dismayed at the injustices that are perpetrated on them. Looking at most of their backgrounds one is faced with abject housing conditions, traumatised births, hospitalisation and all the implications that parental separation (at any early stage) entails, illegitimacy, struggling one-parent families and school refusal coupled with failure in school, presenting such a tapestry of distress that even the most optimistic can only hope to repair and patch. Only the most comprehensive social legislation in all urban areas could help to make this tapestry a work of art and permanent beauty rather than an ever-increasing mural of suffering and anguish. In 90 per cent of cases where the issue is concerned with what are termed inadequate parents, the inadequacy lies in provision. The two most glaring factors here which could make a start towards finding the remedy would be shelter and a total change in attitudes towards the needy by everyone. This demands caring at all levels and to sustain this is not easy.

I cannot but think when I meet such families and children that even recognition of them seems remote; yet recognition has got to be tangible and real if it is to be of any value. Parents need to be valued and children thrive on it – not just patronised adulation within an educational framework – but a valid 'Hello Mark,' or 'I'm glad you're back Jean, is your Mum better?' It seems to me quite alienating for city children to drift into school from impersonalised housing estates or dying basements and enter a class perfunctorily without some sort of personal greeting. I have often looked at the Yale/ Union key ring necklaces that so many children wear – and wondered what they are returning to.

I think of my own infant schooling. It was war-time and Bevin had claimed my coal-mining father all the day and seemingly much of the night. My mother worked evenings driving a crane in a Black Country munitions factory. She arrived home in the early hours of the morning to see me off to school and manage what housework she could. Each lunch-time I returned home to find her laid out on the sofa, still in her overalls, hands stained with grease. Her teeth were in a cup – and the snoring came in blowing and sucking sounds from the collapsed face. She certainly didn't look like the Mums in the reading books at school playing with Janet, John, Dick or Dora. She was neither tidy nor painted and permed. There was usually a note with sixpence on the table : 'Get some chips from Mrs Sherwood.' At times I pestered or prodded her for some reaction – even a hostile one was better than none at all. I arrived home each evening in time to say goodnight to her.

Greeting – the word itself seems to have Victorian connotations – yet its sterility on a Christmas card is almost all that remains of it. Come rain or shine, our children are greeted and it's a ritual which we all enjoy. I am not a Catholic – but I worked in a Catholic primary school for a time and one of the prayers began 'Each new day is a gift from God . . .' In other words, let's get on with it, there's lots to do, we are alive. However, I'd be a fool not to admit I've been glad to see the back of some days, but then again the individual goodnights seem to repair ill-will and ease away tensions and prejudice.

Collective worship and assembly are still a legal obligation in state schools in Britain. There were difficulties here for me – my school age range was from five to seventeen years – subject matter? I did not want departmental assemblies. Nor did I want the assembly to be a hymn, a prayer, a behaviour tirade and out to play. Assemblies in other schools that I had worked in always interested me. I remembered my own time at grammar school – 13-plus entrant. Prefects would marshal us into serried ranks and we stood in classes in the hall – 1a, 1b, 2a, 2b. The masters would file on to the hall platform and form a semicircle and finally the headmaster would take his place in the centre. I suppose there was some theatrical attraction in it. Some of the masters wore their gowns and none of the teachers in my village had ever done that. Miss Craddock wore a flowered smock—but that was in the infants school and Miss Craddock had told me that I was a good reader – and that I might be an actor or a lawyer. She also asked about my Mum and Dad and brother and I haven't forgotten her.

Hymn number 157 – 'Immortal, invisible God only wise . . .' I always felt invisible in those assemblies. The hymn was followed by a prayer. Then something called fortnightly lists were read out. All subjects throughout a two-week period were tested and scored and we competed for the honour of having our name read out.

'Form 1a: first Carroll, second Kingaby, third Lewis. Form 2b: first Harvey, second Dando, third Smith.'

It was usually the same names each week – if you were first you had the increased honour of taking the list out to the headmaster. I think I managed a third or second once in a while, but was moved into an 'A' stream within a year and never got beyond midway after that. By that time I was bored with the whole procedure. Even cheating marks seemed to lose its point for many of us. Perhaps at fourteen we were beginning to mature. There was nothing to look forward to from those assemblies and there was only one which was in any sense dramatic.

A group of boys had been reported to the headmaster for stealing from the local Woolworth's. The goods had all been returned. The headmaster informed us of the dishonour and disgrace it had brought on the school. Then each boy was called on to the stage and bent over. Each boy was lashed across the buttocks, was it four times or six? It seemed endless. One boy yelped after the second lash and jumped from the stage. He was reverently returned to receive his due share.

I have since pondered about those beatings, how they affected us all, the masters, the ten-year-olds, the teenagers, the prefects, the beater and the beaten. I wonder too, now, where the disgrace to the school lies. Is it in the theft, or the beating? In the space of ten years it all seems grotesquely unreal.

At twenty-four I was working with Sybil Williams at Colebrooke Day Maladjusted School in Islington. The school catered for children suffering from emotional disturbances who could not be helped in an ordinary school. Her assemblies were conducted informally via topics and news which the children themselves brought forward. She handled it all marvellously well – gently persuasive as well as being informative. I can still hear her Australian voice now. 'Oh, come on now Clive – be fair, let Doris give her news. Well, it might be boring for you – but others want to hear it, I do for one, so does Barbara and Mr Swann – don't you Mr Swann? Anyway, Doris has listened to you and you've already given three bits of news.' On it went, ranging from the assassination of Kennedy to Doris Jones's mother's drain being blocked up.

I needed something like this in terms of corporate communication. However, the total number of children at Colebrooke School was rarely much above forty. The roll of my own school was over 160, and if the waiting list was any indication, the accommodation looked to be at capacity level for years to come. Routine and some ritual, coupled with spontaneity, needed to be sought after – I had to use the assembly like a builder uses cement. It had to be part of everything, living in the school, the building itself and the community outside. After the first assembly on the day the school opened, I knew that this would not be as difficult as it had appeared in theory.

Apart from being of mixed origin, the children or their parents adhered to many different religions. There were West Indians belonging to the Jehovah's Witnesses or Church of God, Greeks and Turks and Cypriots belonging to Christian Orthodoxy or Islam, Jews, Kosher and non-Kosher, Hindu and Sikh, and Irish Catholics and Protestants who proved by their friendships that the troubles in Ulster had their origin on earth and not in heaven. A visiting social worker asked me once about children of the indigenous population. (What a cooked expression that is: it makes a group of people sound like a left-over portion of steamed pudding.) I thought of the books I had read on the East End and of the rather romanticised ideas about tightly knit communities. I knew this was what she was asking about. These communities were dissolving, but I did not view it with Hampstead or Bloomsbury regret. There were families of the kind she wanted information on, but they were fast disappearing. One could view them with the same nostalgia as looking at an old sepia print. On a religious basis this group were baptised (for the most part) Church of England and that was that.

I was opening a new school which would be practically filled with children on the first day. The children on entering the building must feel that it was theirs. The staff were all appointed before opening, we were not strangers to one another as I had worked with most of them before at other schools and they had followed me to the present situation. The Easter vacation proved invaluable – we had a building, not a school. Photographs were taken of the workmen. Bulldozers were pushing great mounds of earth around; trenches scarred the playground like a battlefield and planks of wood were being hoisted into the air to form a roof. There were

West Indians, Greeks, Irish and Sikhs, all bringing their respective talents to what was to be a multi-racial school. The photographs were displayed throughout the school, with captions: 'People and workers from many different lands all working together to build your school.'

2

SOME FRIENDS,
SOME NEIGHBOURS AND SOME OTHERS

By 21 April, teachers and helpers were ready for the children
– the building itself was not quite finished, in fact the Sikh
carpenter was still working on the roof. I liked the idea of his
being there and the banging and knocking didn't perturb me.
It was like having a living weather vane – I hope the elements
will always be kind to that man. All the children up to the
age of eleven were arriving by coach, coming from no less
than ten different schools, five of which were within the
special school category. We were all as prepared as we possibly
could be, stock and equipment were ready, classrooms were
empty of children but alive with equipment and staff. I
remembered that there were fears about the building not being
ready in time.

The Administrative Officer was speaking: 'Your staffing
is now complete – our only fear is that the building may not
be ready. It is most unfortunate – we do not wish to delay
the opening and this will cause all sorts of difficulties.'

'With this staff I could give you a school if you gave me
nine tents on the playing fields.'

No smile answered my remark, which was not intended to
be facetious.

'There will be no question of that,' came the reply.

In a few minutes the buses were to arrive – in spite of being
prepared there was apprehension, not spoken but felt, and

it was shared by all. Any latent fears were dispersed as the three dark green buses pulled up and the children spilled out. I had made no stipulations with regard to uniforms. Parents and children should decide what is suitable. How is it possible for a child to develop personal tastes in dress if he or she is forced into navy blue or bottle green between the ages of five and sixteen? It should not be necessary for a school to legislate on this point. Our school needed to be part of a community and the children's appearance would inevitably reflect this. If a uniform had been compulsory, then we should have chosen a red, blue, green, yellow, brown or black anorak.

The gaily patterned coats, brightly coloured stockings and fluorescent crocheted ponchos stood out like spring flowers against the half-demolished houses and rubble which faced the entrance of the school. Yet, the faces remain more clear, black, brown, olive, white – complexions of every hue. We greeted them all with smiles and handshakes, adolescents and infants alike. An assembly took place after the children had settled. This corporate meeting had to be successful, it was the beginning of a pattern which would serve as a focal point, proving that all the children were part of the school – they were more important than the bricks and mortar, more important than the staff. The school was theirs and this they must know and feel. I never believed that this idea could be beyond a child's conception – and the ensuing years bore this out.

Before any classes were sent for, seating was carefully arranged in the hall and music and hymns were to be sorted out. I chose the following song to see us all in: 'If I needed a neighbour, were you there? Were you there? If I needed a neighbour were you there? And the creed and the colour and the name won't matter, were you there? Were you there?' Hymns were bound to be a problem – this was easily solved, the teachers were in good voice and all of them sang. Children entered accompanied by piano and guitar. We sang it twice and the second time all the children joined in and as they sang some of the bewilderment disappeared from their faces and the smiles became infectious. It was going to be all right. We were neighbours, and we were there. From this day onwards, our assembly was to be much more than a routine and a ritual, it was to be an integral part of us all and had to be planned accordingly. There was not much to say on that first day, the children were strangers to us and children judge adults by what they do, not necessarily by what they say, which is fair enough. 'Praise God from whom all blessings flow, praise Him ye creatures here below, praise Him above . . .' and the school day passes for many a child without so much as a glimmer of that particular commodity that even God finds helpful. I praised them for the way they had entered, for looking so attractive, said how happy I was to see them all and how all of us had so much looked forward to meeting them. The teachers, men and women, were introduced to the children in the hall there and then and were given bunches of daffodils by the children. There was no embarrassment on receiving them, the teachers needed to belong too and the flowers (which were a surprise to them) were more important and integrating than any textbook or lecture on inter-disciplinary management.

As the weeks sped by, assemblies developed into joyful gatherings. Like the seasons, they were changeable. Under present ministry regulations, religious education is compulsory. What was I to do about prayers, with no less than fourteen different faiths or beliefs represented? On the face of it, this would appear to be impossible to deal with on a collective basis and certainly the school could not split into fourteen different prayer-gatherings every day. Depressed children in school (and there were many of them) gave me a simple solution. This statement was our prayer.

'For a short time I want you to wish, hope or pray, it might be for yourself, or for a friend, or for your Mum or Dad, or even someone you have never met. Can you do that for me? Thank you.'

Stories of every kind were told – not read – and fairy stories took on a strange light when children improvised and acted the stories after their telling. Here is the beginning of their version of Cinderella.

Stepmother: 'What you think you been doing all day sitting here starin'? Where is Bentley and Merva? I told you to look after them. Where are they now?'

'Playing, something gone wrong with the paraffin heater – it smoked and I had to take it outside. I don't know where those two have gone.'

'You don't know nothin'. I thought I told you to clean the kitchen. Did you go up to the rent office to pay the money?'

'I forget it.'

'Forget it? (Cinderella is slapped.) I work hard all day for you, my back ache with packing boxes and you forget. You no help, no use to me. I feed, clothe you, you give me no help. Don't you sit there no more my girl, you move yourself. (Another slap.) Here take this to the bag-wash and waste no time and find Merva and Bentley.'

'Mammy – can I go to the club dancing on Saturday?'

'Dance, where you think I have money for dancin'? You dance here if you want to dance.' (Cinderella begins to cry.) 'No sense in cryin', I ain't got no time to cry, you get your-self to the bag-wash and here (gives Cinderella some money) bring me a loaf and two bottles of milk on your way home.'

Cinderella leaves the house and sits down on a bench and begins to cry again.

Enter a lady accompanied by a young man: 'What's wrong, why you sit here cryin'?'

'I am sad, I cry, I don't care about nothin' . . .'

The content and language of their interpretation of these stories told me so much about their lives. How far the mirror was an exaggeration I don't know. I do know that when

Prince Charming does come along, it will be highly unlikely that he will have riches or a palace to take them to, perhaps not even a home. I also knew that all the children needed something real to look forward to; fantasy was not enough. Birthdays were never missed, always celebrated by a present and applause. If children wished, this could take place in class or even privately, but most of them opted for an assembly-time ovation. Forthcoming events of the day were discussed, also of the next week, month, and so on until a continuous kaleidoscope was presented of visits, happenings, and achievement; reinforcements of successes, however small, were never left out. Children's work was shown regularly and praise and applause were constant throughout. Praise can be delivered individually and collectively from teachers; applause from other children is just as spontaneous as the wretched booing witnessed at football matches. However, it needs to be cultivated. Without applause, appreciation and praise, criticism, sanctions and discipline all become meaningless to depressed and underprivileged children and any creativity or natural histrionics that they may possess can only be expressed in fracturing or destroying the school day that is offered.

We have really said goodbye to Mr Chips because no one teacher (by the sheer goodness of his frame) is going to aid such children to lasting positive social adjustments. The orchestra must play together to attain a symphony, and solo and virtuoso performances by teachers, parents, social workers and all other agencies are only going to be of use if they are part of it.

Visits out of the school gave us all a chance to play in tune. Each class made one visit of particular interest each week, ranging from motor-component factories, a cosmetics factory, clothing factories and museums of every nature to Epping Forest and adventure playgrounds. Once a year the whole school embarked on a day out. Organising transport for 168 children, parents and teachers, is rather like the 'Wagons

West' preparation one sees in a western. There are sandwiches to be made, drinks to organise, insurance, timing, spare underpants, sanitary towels, first aid boxes and a thousand other things to be thought of. Somehow it all gets sorted out by the time the day arrives.

We had worked out a visit of multiple interest that would suit all the children. We were to travel by coach to Westminster Pier and take the boat down the river to Greenwich; then split into groups, visiting the *Cutty Sark*, the Observatory, the boating pool and then the playing fields and adventure playground, all followed by a picnic lunch and then home.

It was a rare, clear September morning; parents, helpers and children were all packed into the buses. A last-minute check showed we hadn't forgotten anything. We were ready to leave.

'Tom – telephone.'

'Oh, not now, we're just ready to leave – ask if it's urgent.'

'It's Mrs Timms – she says it is urgent.'

I hurried back into the office, cursing because I was holding up the outing and the children were getting impatient.

'Hello.' I spoke brusquely.

'Oh, hello Mr Wakefield, it's Mrs Timms 'ere. I don't want to worry yer but it's about Delroy.'

'Yes, what is it?'

'I've 'ad a 'phone-call to say someone's goin' to kill him. I didn't want him to miss the outin', he's so full of it. I don't want to talk to the police about it; it's private, but I thought I ought to let you know, OK?'

Afterwards all I could hear was the gentle purring of the telephone. It did not soothe me. I looked at it almost as though it might respond and give me the correct coded answer. One of the local vicars was accompanying us; he had always helped in all capacities, never sanctimonious, always practical and good.

'John, I want you stay with Delroy all day. Not to leave his side – not an instant, you understand.'

'Yes, but is that all? I'd like to be of more help.'

'Someone may try to kill him today – it might be just a nasty scare. It might be true.'

'Oh.' There was less than a second's hesitation. 'Yes, of course.'

There was no time for a corporate decision, no time for a staff meeting. The permission for Delroy to go on the trip and all the heavy pending responsibilities were mine.

'You're sure he should go, Tom?'

'Yes, keep that young social worker with you too.'

I went to look at Delroy; he seemed fine and in good form.

'Can I have some candy floss at Greenwich, Miss Rishworth is going to take me on a big ship, I've got 12p to spend . . .'

His speech defect didn't hold his ideas back – nor would any-one take this day from him, that was certain. I felt in my right-hand pocket to check if I had the phenobarbitone which some children were dosed with (Delroy being one of them). A last glance round, a wave to the first of the coach-drivers and we were off. As we were leaving, a huge crane swung what seemed to be half a house across the sky. It seemed odd that this great block of concrete dangling in the sky above us before we left was destined to be someone's home. A few more waves from well-wishers, songs coming from the coaches, clouds of dust erupting from the unfinished roads and we were gone.

The day was idyllic and as we sailed down the Thames singing and looking at buildings and listening to the yelping and grinding cranes on the riverway, witnessing a whole city in the state of metamorphosis, I realised that all I could think of that day was my responsibility and accountability for Delroy. There was one very bad moment, which occurred as we were leaving the boat. Delroy and the vicar were separated from my view in the hustle to disembark. Then I saw them standing on the quayside. Above them, staring intently, was a rather stricken-looking man in a long black overcoat, practically reaching his heels. Numb with concern, I watched him descend the iron steps and make his way towards them. I pushed my way past children and parents, trod on boxes of sandwiches, got myself down the gang-plank and somehow managed to place myself in between the black overcoat and Delroy and the vicar. The overcoat was clearly alarmed.

'What do you want?' I demanded.

'What d'yer mean, what do I want? You don't think you can get off this bleedin' pier without a ticket do yer?'

'Oh here.' I proffered the piece of paper which accounted for us being there. He took it, looked at me as if he were very sorry for my state of mind, and ambled away. I was too relieved to apologise. The rest of the time at Greenwich and the journey home was full of fun and interest, yet that telephone call left me curiously detached throughout the day's proceedings. On arriving home that night. I felt very old and tired. The telephone rang several times – some of the parents were thanking me for a lovely day.

3

JUST HERBERT

An open policy had always been adopted towards parents
and they could come into school whenever they liked. After
a time they did come – sometimes to talk about themselves,
sometimes about their children, either was valid. Some of
them worked in school with us as helpers or attendants and
their good sense and warmth proved beyond price. Parent
meetings after school were numerous and valuable in content.
At times, we presented entertainment, socials, dances and
pantomimes, which seemed to lighten the tedium of so many
of their lives. There were meetings devoted entirely to discussions with teachers and parents concerning their children
and themselves. In spite of the hardship many of these families
had suffered, most responded to our efforts with goodwill and
what support their means could offer. No official parental
committee was acceptable to them for they were hostile to
forms and committees – a hostility which, for many of them,
was reinforced with a fundamental distrust of authority.
Clothing could have been a problem : many parents were too
proud to fill in forms or accept a visit from the Education
Welfare Officer and were very loathe to use the clothing
voucher at the Co-op. A huge cupboard in my room, marked
'files', was full of shoes, underpants, vests, pullovers of all
sizes and so on. Mothers in real need could be helped at any
time without any questions or social sanctions. The clothing

had come from many firms (my secretary was always corresponding with them) and was in excellent condition. No parent ever abused this service and its individual usage was known only to me and the parent involved.

From this, one should not dismiss the work of the Education Welfare Officer who visited families and also stayed with us in school two days each week. Hazel Block cared passionately (I'm sorry, it's the only way to describe her). One of the teachers once said of her: 'Hazel doesn't explain to families how they could manage without a cooker, nor does she analyse why the kitchen is in so much of a mess. She cleans the kitchen and gets them a cooker.'

That summarises a very remarkable woman. Hazel, the school doctor and our speech therapist were school-based and I feel that the psychological services, if they are to be of any real use, should also follow this pattern. Otherwise appointments will continue to be broken and the help that the psychological services have to offer (and I do feel they can help many) is about as much use as an empty office block.

A set of papers had been dropped on my desk with these words scrawled across: 'Not suitable for child guidance – exclusion pending if admission to ESN school is not swift.' I needn't have looked at the papers – the school was already full. Then I noticed the age of the child – almost fourteen. It had taken a very long time for someone to decide that he was educationally sub-normal. Herbert Larenthe – born St Lucia – arrived in this country to join mother . . . I was driven on by curiosity. He had been here for less than a few months and had been placed in a large comprehensive school. His IQ, tested on the Stanford Binet, stood at 52 (very low) and his behaviour was described as 'noisy and aggressive'. He had one year left of his school life and unless I took him in, that might be spent in exclusion from school with an hour a day of home tuition if he was lucky. But what could we do for him in a year? I was not optimistic, yet I couldn't put the papers

away in the filing cabinet. It would be like burying the boy.
'Hello, yes, could you give me special school placement,
please? Hello, Linda, this boy Herbert Larenthe. I am inter-
viewing him for admittance, can you arrange the appointment
please?'

'Oh, yes, I'm so relieved. I thought I'd never place him, his
age and everything . . . next Thursday at 10.30 am – OK?'

'Yes – bye.'

There were already a lot of aggressive children in the school
and roughly they split into three main types – there were
noisy, outgoing extroverts, there were attention-seeking, pro-
vocatively aggressive children and what can only be termed
withdrawn, hostile children. It was more than difficult to
attempt to meet all their needs, but we tried. Praise helped,
but certain groupings and classroom methods also assisted
such children, both socially and educationally. Before I
attempt to go into any theories on method, let me say at once
that I feel it is imperative for all teachers to have background
and experience of infant technique. One of the saddest aspects
of education today is the number of teachers in secondary
schools who feel that infant education is merely play.

Solitary play is, in fact, one of the simplest forms of educational activity – a child investigating for his own satisfaction. So when little Peter (a 'pram' child who has never had
a chance of this kind of play in his life) pulls a leg or an arm
off his action man doll, he is not necessarily being destructive
but may be merely having a closer look. Toys for infants need
to be flexible. Looking at young children play, I am always
impressed by the satisfaction it gives. Aggressive and difficult
children find sharing very hard indeed and stimuli must
initially be presented for them alone. They need, essentially,
to do it for themselves and not to share. The praise and
adulation must go solely to them and they must be allowed to
wallow in it. This is not to say that they will not continue to
negate suggestions and even wreck what they do – but when

presentation and encouragement are consistent they do, in most cases, accept and benefit from some of it. Apart from this, such children would seek to ruin the work of groups of other children involved in parallel, sharing or competitive ways of learning. At least these children and their teacher are given some respite during solitary play periods.

Timing in our class-teaching situation was vital to any form of presentation and it seemed asinine to project children into working situations for which they were not socially or emotionally ready. If they had managed solitary play successfully, then parallel play would appear to be the next natural form of educational growth process. Here we had children working together on a similar activity but not actually sharing what they did. The more difficult the child, the more careful the gradation had to be. Let him have his own pencil, colours, named if necessary – 'Yes, John, that's your bit . . .' – separate yet subtly collective.

'Jean, tell Clare that I am very pleased with her picture, the colours are lovely. Ask her if I can put it on the wall next to your flowers.' Wait for a time and you might get an answer through your go-between.

'Clare says she wants to change her picture and no she doesn't want it on the wall.' Perhaps not the most vigorous of responses but there is a beginning, even if it constitutes rejecting the praise and a chance of group participation.

Eventually, parallel play led to sharing play which is a basis for all civilised existence. Communication and total development must feed on it, but many children are not introduced to it sufficiently well, resulting, often, in a lasting social handicap explained away as some neurosis or another. Obviously our teaching needed to be creative in this field. There was always a great deal of music and drama and art, the building continuously reverberated with songs (thank God for the West Indian voices) and the art and craft in the building was displayed everywhere. This did not mean that there was a dependency on specialised subjects. How often have I heard of some children being 'released' through 'psycho-drama' or music therapy – for how long? This is not in any way meant to denigrate what is being done in these particular fields. On the contrary, they have proved that feelings as well as intellect need nurture. It is for the class teacher to appraise and follow consistently, possibly a much more difficult job as the class teacher cannot afford too much variation in per-formance.

As far as possible, our grouping of children was on an emotional/intellectual/social basis rather than a chronological one. One can feel and act seventy yet only be seventeen – yet our schooling years are still clearly and sharply defined into stages which still (for the most part) are adapted to age. One other play aspect that I must mention always provided us with the most problems. This was competitive play. If children are to enter the working world, then inevitably they are going to be subjected to competition – much of it painful, much of it the major cause of mental illness and crime throughout the country, but it's here and it looks as though it's here to stay. Sadly, it followed that we had to give some form of com-petitive learning (with all the false euphoria and suffering involved) to provide our leavers with the necessary amount of resilience they needed to face the future. However, it still remained clear to us that if our children were forced to com-pete before they were ready then we could expect little from them but sullen response, organised submission and next to nothing in terms of valid achievement.

According to Herbert's mother, his record of achievement in London had been negligible since his arrival. She sat in the armchair in my office; there were two bags, one full of shopping, the other destined for the launderette. A small half-sister of Herbert's was enjoying herself on the rocking horse, oblivious to Mrs Larenthe's complaints or Herbert's obvious discomfort and tension. He was tall, black, very attractive and sat perched nervously on the edge of his chair. Most of the time he stared at the floor during his mother's tirade, occasionally he would rub his hands together and then look up and shake his head. I did not know whether these were gestures of defeat, defiance or disagreement. Whatever the issue, the boy was suffering and I could bear it no longer.

Mrs Larenthe was speaking: 'I leave the alarm for him and still he stay in bed, he late for school, sometime he miss school. A lady come round my house from the Office – she say your boy Herbert not in school. I ask him why you not in school. This all he do – shake his head.'

I cut into the conversation: 'I like your shirt Herbert, it suits you. Did you choose it yourself?'

'I buy it in Ridley Road Market, there are many clothes there.'

This was not the response of a dull adolescent.

'Did you like your last school?'

'It was OK,' he replied without any feeling.

'If you would like to come here, I think you might enjoy it. We have youth clubs, socials, holidays by the sea. We have more older girls than boys, they are very pretty. We need a boy like you, do you want to give it a try here?'

His answer seemed a long time in coming. The younger sister had become bored with the rocking horse so I had pushed a lollipop into her hand.

'Yes, I come here.' The words were shot out.

'When would you like to start?'

He hunched his shoulders, and held his hands out in a question mark which said, 'You tell me.'

'You can start now, I'll order your dinner and you can meet your teacher and the others in your class. I know you'll like it here and you can really help us, we do need you.'

By this time Mrs Larenthe had assembled her bags, collected the little girl and was standing ready to leave.

'Please contact me if things are difficult at home – you can come here any time. We will help you all we can, here is the telephone number.'

She smiled a tired smile and turned hurriedly away; there was the launderette to do, Bernice to get to school and she had already missed a morning's work.

Within three weeks, Herbert belonged with us; and as his sense of security increased so did his self-expression. He was noisy and often disruptive, but he never lied and never ever bullied or hurt anyone to my knowledge. It was not teachers, helpers or me that seemed to stabilise him and make him aware of his identity. It was a friendship with another boy – Michael. This boy had entered the school a year before as an emergency admission on the grounds of continued school refusal. On admittance he was in a sorry state, nervously debilitated and under treatment at the hospital. He had ugly bald patches on his head where great tufts of hair had fallen out, this alopecia being a testament to his nervous condition. His Irish mother was a warm, concerned woman who already had great problems in that her eldest daughter was totally paralysed and permanently home-bound. Within a year of joining us, Michael was thriving. The alopecia had gone, the nervous debility was non-existent. We were confronted with a quiet, confident boy who demanded respect by personal definition. For some reason, Herbert chose this boy as his friend and Michael's influence proved permanent and positive.

I was happy that the staff had decided against a prefect system; all the children were helpers at some time, whatever their age or condition. Aggressive children need responsibility and how could one possibly give this if all responsibility in the building was geared to what we considered a pupil elite and, in the long term, what would that responsibility do to the elite? It was very moving indeed to watch Michael and Herbert helping the reception class at meal-times; they were kindly, humorous and firm and were adored by the smaller children. I wonder if anyone apart from these children had ever respected Herbert before. The staff were beginning to – and he knew it. His intellectual progress grew as his confidence in himself became stronger. There were no special methods indulged, yet he became avid to learn and his reading age soared.

There were funny moments which we could never forget. Margaret Gates (my deputy head) greeted me one morning just after school had started.

'Have you seen Herbert today? Wait till you do.' She smiled wisely and tenderly. 'He looks a knock-out.'

The telephone was ringing and I didn't think any more about it.

At ten o'clock, I would always go round the classes to say hello to children and staff and share in their activities. I passed Herbert in the corridor on his way to cookery class – at least I thought it was Herbert.

I turned round and called, 'Herbert, is that you?'

He faced me squarely and looked directly towards me. 'Yes, it's me all right.'

He was wearing a blue and white striped apron over his flared trousers and pullover and plonked securely on his head was a golden crown. I rocked with laughter and he joined in.

'What's it for? It's not Christmas yet, are you doing a play with Miss Reid?'

'No, we cooking breakfasts, but I'm the king.'

He kept that crown on all day and no one in the school suggested he should take it off. For all of us, the cardboard crown did not symbolise power, it was a manifestation of how Herbert felt; secure, happy and the world was his as much as anyone else's, and what is more, he was happy to share it.

He did give me some difficult moments. Four months before he was due to leave, a note was slipped on to my desk: 'Herbert has run out of school – he's in a furious temper.'

There had been some kind of confrontation with his teacher, I think about noise. Usually if children ran out of school, our policy was to wait. If it happened (and it was rare when it did) it was usually younger children, who would hover round the building – or even tap on my window when they had collected themselves. On no occasions had anyone ever wandered far from the base; truancy was practically nil and there was not a child on probation in the whole school.

Public reaction to disturbed behaviour had always intrigued me. I suppose it is something like the reaction to mental illness, closely connected with people's fears about themselves. Six years before I had accompanied a group of twenty physically handicapped children on a week's school holiday spent on the Kent coast. We were all ambling along the beach at Folkestone, eight of the children in wheelchairs and the rest of them moving only slowly and with the greatest difficulty. Within an hour, no less than three people had pressed over three pounds into my hand: 'Get something for the children.'

The sympathy was real enough; yet in almost all instances where the general public witness disturbed behaviour one gets either over-intensified alarm coupled with tut-tut-tutting, or staring or a 'what's going to happen next?' attitude. Sympathy for all kinds of mental or emotional disturbance must extend further than selling paper flags – particularly in view of the fact that at the present rate of increase in mental illness, no family of four is going to escape it in some form or another. If someone has lost a leg, or an arm, it's simple to feel constructively sorry, because the loss is tangible, but viewing and helping someone emotionally disorientated, whose behaviour might appear to be anti-social, does not come easily to 'Mrs Brown' or 'Colonel Pickering'.

I decided not to leave Herbert to make his own way back to us. Somehow I felt he wanted me to fetch him. He had run in the direction of the playing fields so I put on my overcoat and left the building as unobtrusively as possible. The fields

were inundated with children from other schools playing
football or rounders and I scanned each group to see if Herbert
had joined them. It was much worse than trying to find a
friend on a busy railway station. Just on the point of giving
up, I noticed a lone figure at the far end of the fields standing
in the middle of a roped-off section, probably destined to
become a cricket pitch for the summer months. I walked
slowly towards the figure and noticed that several adults had
gathered around him as though he were in an arena, I got to
the edge of the pitch and let Herbert see me. He was muttering
and cursing and kicking the turf with his foot. The casual
spectators were looking for a climax – it never came.

'I ain't comin' with you.'

'I'm not asking you to. I thought you might want to talk
to me, that's all. Anyway, you're much bigger than me, you
don't expect me to carry you, do you?'

There was a semblance of a smile and the cursing decreased
to mutterings and these finally stopped, leaving him silent
and standing quite still. He had made a gesture; now it was my
turn. I clambered over the ropes, took his arm and led him to
the tea pavilion. His relief was greater than mine and I was
pleased that we had given the onlookers a poor show. Two
teas settled the issue and he returned without bother.

He left school in the August. That wicked old IQ test had
zoomed to 90 from 50, he was found to be no longer in need
of special education and now has a very good job in a chair-
making factory. He reads the papers, attends evening classes
and youth clubs and faces the future with confidence. His
own version of his childhood he related to me later. His
mother had left him at five years of age in St Lucia, in his
grandmother's care.

'I was playin' near the sheds and some kids come runnin'
to me and say to me "Your granny, she dead."

'I say, "You foolin'." Then my auntie come cryin' and say,
"Herbert, your granny dead."

'I ran back to the house and she lyin' there with a towel round her face. I didn't know what to do. Then I stay with my auntie and then my Mammy send for me to come to London.

'Oh boy I never been in an aeroplane before, I never been anywhere but St Lucia. When I get off the 'plane, this lady came to me and say: "You Herbert Larenthe? Well I'm your mother." '

He was thirteen years of age at the time and the rest of his story you have heard. He sees us often still, calls into school on Friday afternoons (his afternoon off) and continues with evening classes and clubs. The friendship with Michael has overlapped the school years. I heard him talking to Michael during one evening class.

'One of the men at work say to me – why don't you go back to your own country?'

Michael spoke without looking up from the piece of wood he was measuring: 'Take no bleedin' notice of him.'

Herbert shrugged, 'I not care, I say this is my country.'

After hearing this conversation I came to the smug conclusion that all would be well with Herbert now that he could move on and make his own way. He was happy in his job and he had good friends. My hopes were premature and probably unrealistic. Two months later he called round at my home at four in the afternoon. He said that he had called just to say 'hello'. At six o'clock he was still with us and I had to explain to him that I was going to the cinema with my friend Rosie from next door.

'Can I come with you? I don't feel like dancin' tonight.'

Rosie must have picked up the urgency behind the question, and the three of us crawled into her Mini all set for two and a half hours with Dr Zhivago. An hour and a quarter went by before Herbert decided that we all needed sustenance to get us through the rest of the film – the theme music had failed to chloroform us or sustain our interest. He disappeared for ten minutes and returned with hamburgers, drinks and chocolates and, like many of the audience, we ate our way through the rest of the film. Herbert presented his bill to us in the foyer of the cinema as we were leaving.

'I can't go home.'

'Why not?' said Rosie.

'Becos' I ain't got nowhere, the door is locked and they won't let me in. They don't want me there. They won't open the door for me.'

'Have you had a row, would you like me to come with you?'

'Yes, you come and see, I don't tell you lies.'

It was ten o'clock, it had begun to drizzle and the streets of East London were void of life as we approached the new maisonette where Herbert lived. Rosie remained in the car and I climbed the stone stairways which led to Herbert's front door. He tried his key in the lock and I tried it also; the catch was on and entrance was impossible.

'Are your parents in, Herbert?' I whispered.

He nodded and pointed to the kitchen light. I knocked on the door and as I did so he moved from the entrance and stood in an alcove reserved for rubbish bins. There was no response to my knocking, except that the kitchen light went out and I could distinctly hear movement and some whispering from within. Herbert looked at me and raised his eyes as if to say 'You see what I mean.'

Whatever the trouble, I didn't want to see him cowering amongst the rubbish bins much longer. I banged on the door and tapped the windows of the maisonette. This at least bore results. I could hear more mutterings and movement and the door was opened six inches, revealing Herbert's mother clad in dressing gown and muslin turban.

'Hello, Mrs Edwards, I'm Herbert's old headmaster. You remember me, don't you?' I felt older as the door opened a little wider. 'Is Herbert's stepfather at home?'

There was no reaction to this question, it was blandly ignored.

'Herbert, he in trouble?' she asked. I had the distinct
feeling that she hoped he might be.

'No, of course not, he's not that sort of boy. He could be in
trouble though, if he's locked out all night. Can I come in
and talk about this? Herbert is with me, can he . . .?'

'He stay where he is; yes do, please come in.'

I looked at Herbert and his nod gave me an assurance that
he would wait. The maisonette was scrupulously clean. The
linoleum in the hall reflected my shoes as Mrs Edwards led
me into the lounge. The room was thickly carpeted with a
heavy floral design; on top of the carpet were placed, at
orderly intervals, four orange and white fluffy nylon rugs. The
rest of the furnishing consisted of a heavy velveteen three-
piece suite, a covered velvet stool and three grandiose coffee-
tables. No dust was to be seen anywhere and there was not
the slightest semblance of disorder; it could have been the
window display of a furnishing store. I found it hard to believe
that three young children besides Herbert lived in this house.

The orderliness of it all was further emphasised by the
ornamentation, which regimented the room to an even greater
degree than the furnishings. Tiny dolls, chalk-china figures.
dotted the shelves, tables and sideboard. The ashtrays remained
unused as did the plastic fruit, plastic flowers and plastic
vegetables which not only graced the tables, but also hung
from the walls. It was May, yet Christmas cards were neatly
hung in a line across one wall. Everything had its allotted
place and there was so much to keep in place – wall and
floor-space would appear to be exhausted by this description,
yet even more space was taken up by photographs. They were
everywhere and of every kind, some suspended from the walls
and others placed in elaborate frames. Posed groups and indi-
viduals stared from all directions. I scanned them for a glimpse
of Herbert, but he was not to be seen. Near my head was a
coloured film portrayal of Jesus Christ and written under-
neath was something like 'God is looking' or 'God is watching'

– I can't quite remember what He was supposed to be doing.

I opened the conversation cautiously and complimented Mrs Edwards with regard to her home. She responded warmly to my praise and I decided to talk about Herbert, who was still waiting outside. At the mention of his name the warmth disappeared, but she remained composed.

'I ask him to do the laundry on Saturday morning before I go out to work, I wake him at half past seven in the morning, but no he stay in bed till nine, then he go off to play football. He no help to me that boy. On Saturday nights he not get in till eleven o'clock of an evenin'. I tired of him. He give me five pounds a week and he expect to come and go as he please . . .'

'Well Herbert works hard now, he never stays away from work, he gets up at half past six in the morning and is working by eight. He tells me he works overtime two nights a week, so he might be a bit tired by the time Saturday morning comes. Most London boys of sixteen like to go to the dance of a Saturday, Mrs Edwards, and there are not many of them that are in by eleven. What about tonight? This door was bolted at ten-fifteen. You wouldn't want him to stay out on the streets all night, would you?'

My question was answered with a shrug.

'He no help to me, no help at all.'

'What would you like him to do, apart from paying good board? If he agrees to do the laundry, will you agree not to lock him out any more? Can I call him in and we can all talk about it together?'

She agreed and I beckoned for Herbert to come in. He entered apprehensively and did not sit down, but stood and looked at the floor. I cannot record my conversational webs of conciliation, the emptiness of my verbal paper-patching of emotional rejections and fissures which I could not hope to bridge or mend. I left after Herbert had agreed to do the laundry one evening each week and his mother had promised not to lock him out again. She also promised me that she would telephone me at work or at home if she did contemplate doing it. Mother and son shook hands and the Lord of Heaven stared in silent beatific witness from the wall. I left quickly and climbed into the Mini next to Rosie.

'Are you all right?' she asked, as she opened the engine.

I wanted to talk about something else, the film, our adjacent gardens or her forthcoming holiday in Persia. It was not until we were speeding homewards through the dark and drizzle that, like his mother and stepfather, I realised that I too was putting Herbert in abeyance. I was trying to forget him.

No such escapism was allowed – little more than two months later, on a Saturday evening at home when television had been abandoned for the Scrabble board, the front door bell buzzed. It was 11.30 and as I walked along the corridor I saw two eyes peering at me through the letterbox. He stood there, moving from one foot to the other, extremely agitated. He spoke before I could begin.

'It's no use, I ain't goin' back there, no I'm never goin' back. They don't want me. They tell me to go and take the key from me. Don't ask me to go back 'cos I ain't goin'. Can I stay here tonight? She tell me to get a room, but it's too dark to look for one now. He take the key from me. I got nowhere to go.'

There didn't seem much use in trying to reason with him. There was a small spare room vacant. I made him a cup of tea and gave him a bacon sandwich and decided to talk over the situation the next day, after he had slept. I couldn't force him to go home and neither could I let him roam the streets. I think he knew that he had presented me with an ultimatum and furthermore I think he knew that circumstance would force me to accept it. He took the transistor radio up to the spare room and we could hear him singing accompaniments to the pop songs. Before our Scrabble game had ended the pop songs had faded and we assumed that Herbert was sleeping.

Sunday morning is always a wallowing time for me, cups of tea and the papers in bed leave me in a hippopotamus-like state of bliss. On this particular Sunday, the planned sojourn was denied me. I was awoken by a rhythmic clicking noise. I turned over in bed hoping that I could find deeper mud and block out the noise. The clicking and clacking continued. It was no use – I got up, washed and dressed quickly. The bathroom window was open and I gazed out on to the garden, half-shaved, half-awake. My lawn was now only three-quarters of a wilderness. Herbert was snapping his way through the dandelions and tall tufts of coarse grass with the garden shears. This practical 'thank you' broke my torpor; I finished shaving quickly and joined him in the garden. I began weeding and he told me that he had made himself some tea and toast, then gave me a stricture on the state of the lawn.

'It's no good you growing flowers round the side if the middle no good.' Then he seized a clump of dandelions and tore them out. 'These flowers are bad, they change to clocks and the wind blow them everywhere, they take over everything.'

He continued hacking at the grass and talked on about the misfortunes of Chelsea and the latest John Wayne film.

'Herbert, you know we will have to go over to your home today. I will have to talk to your Mum and Dad; I have to, you know that don't you?'

He attacked the grass with fresh vigour and seemed to make the shears move twice as quickly as before.

'Yes, I know,' he replied without stopping.

'Rosie will take me over in the car. I think it will be better if you come with us, would you?'

He stopped working and took a long adult look at me.

'OK, but it's no use you know.'

Within an hour I was repeating the door knocking, window tapping operation of the previous time. However, this time Herbert and Rosie stood on either side of me at the front door.

Eventually it was opened by Mr Edwards. I had not met him before.

'Hello, Mr Edwards, I am . . .' the same conversation ensued. '. . . Would you mind if I came in to talk about it? This is my girlfriend.'

He was pleasant, but cautious. 'Yes, yes you do come in, she too, but Herbert no, he stay out.'

Herbert took up his usual position in the recess and Rosie and I were ushered in. We heard children's footsteps on the stairs, but there was no sign of them or Mrs Edwards when we entered the lounge. I was given no opportunity of presenting Herbert's case, his stepfather began talking even before we could sit down.

'Nice to meet you, but he is not coming here any more, not inside this house, not inside my house. I don't want to see him any more, his mother don't wish to see him.'

'Has he been a bad boy? He says he helps with the shopping and does the laundry, he only stays out late of a Saturday, I . . .'

Mr Edwards didn't want to hear. 'He's not a bad boy I know, outside he's no trouble, but I don't want him here, he's no good here. You take him away thank you, find him a room, he cannot stay here. This week he only give his mother ten pounds, I ask him for all the wages, the other seven. I give him some pocket money, but no, he says he needs seven pounds for clothes.'

It was clear that Herbert's board had rocketed well past any price rises. He was giving his parents ten pounds a week out of his wages of seventeen pounds. From his seven pounds over, he had to buy all his own clothes and his mid-day meal. Mr Edwards broke into my angry internal mathematics.

'He is no use to us, he say it's not fair when I ask him for all his wages, ten pounds is all his mother get.'

I controlled my anger, in fact I diverted it.

'Would you mind if I smoked Mr Edwards?' At least I'd

have the satisfaction of mucking up an untarnished ashtray. I had decided that there was to be no more dialogue with this man who seemed to regard his stepson as a unit trust, or an investment property. Looking at it in these financial terms, he hadn't done badly; Herbert had only left school a year ago, since when he had contributed five pounds to the household from the onset of his working life and this figure had doubled by the time he was sixteen. If remuneration to one's family is the price of being born, then the only debt Herbert owed to anyone was to his grandmother.

Mr Edwards stood, indicating that the situation was closed for him and Rosie gave me a worried-looking glance. I answered both gestures by lighting another cigarette.

'Of course, Herbert will need his clothes, he has two good suits (teachers had provided him with these) and he will need his working clothes, all his shirts, shoes and stockings – you do have them here don't you?'

They must have been at hand, for he left the room and dumped them in a pile outside the kitchen door. No container of any kind was provided, not even a plastic bag.

'Yes, thank you, you take these things, put him in a room, we don't want to see him.'

Rosie stared at the jumble of clothes in disbelief, as if to say, 'Is this all there is to everything?'

I could hear voices upstairs and this bald callousness gave me fresh courage.

'Herbert had a post office savings book while he was at school, he'd better have that too, as I know he tries to save a little each week.'

The savings book was produced from a drawer and I pocketed it without further ceremony. Rosie had begun to fold some of the clothes over her arms. I called to Herbert for help in carrying them, but he was barred entrance and we passed shoes and underwear to him by way of a human chain. He whispered something to Rosie and she passed the message on to me.

'Oh, and can we have his transistor radio and his two records and the football books?'

These increased Herbert's assets and spurred Mr Edwards to greater urgency in delivering his farewells to me.

'Thank you, goodbye.'

'I will give you Herbert's address in case you might want to see him.'

'No, I don't want it, you see to all that.'

'I will call next week and let you know how he is settled.'

'Yes, if you want to, but we are not worried for him.'

Two little girls had peeped round the stairway; Herbert's mother had not been able to contain them upstairs any longer.

I smiled, 'Are these your daughters, they're very pretty?' Inwardly I wanted to say something wounding to Mr Edwards, but nothing came out. I nodded and smiled, he did likewise and the front door closed. Herbert and Rosie had taken his belongings into the Mini and were waiting for me. On my way down, I picked up one of his football stockings which had been dropped in transit and carried it with me to the car. Many times I have read the word 'deprivation', many times had I discussed the facets of the word and the implication of its real meaning, but holding the solitary stocking brought its proper meaning sharply into focus for me for the very first time.

Herbert, at the time of writing, is staying with neighbours. He has made his room his home and calls round almost every week. He enjoys his work and is popular within the firm; and slowly, he is making his own family roots in his relationships. Perhaps one day he will write the rest of his story himself – it wouldn't surprise me if he did. What does surprise me is the number of children who, like Herbert, defeat the odds stacked against them; and what appals me is the treatment of, and provision for, those who don't.

4

THE QUIET ONES ARE NO TROUBLE

It would be romantic to think that all the children had such a success or partial-success story as Herbert, or to convey the idea that all of us, staff and children, were joyful all of the time. The magnitude of the task involved in the teaching of our children must by now be apparent to the reader. Each day confronted us with something else that we were not doing. It soon became obvious to me that there was no alternative to involvement and it was essential for helpers and teachers to take some stock of their own wear and tear in the process. Some analysis needed to be made as to our own equilibrium and sense of proportion if we were to maintain the consistency and the insight needed to help such children. When these factors were upset, then we suffered and so did the children. No matter how balanced a teacher, no matter how well-prepared or organised, he or she must at some time suffer from the stress that many of the pupils were afflicted with.

Stress usually occurs where there is a split or conflict between inner wishes and impulses on one side and the actual external or classroom situation on the other. Often, it is just reduced to inner urges and one's own conscience. Within the classroom situation many teachers realise what they need to do. They know what they can do. Yet they suffer from stress because what they do achieve is too much of a compromise for their own consciences to accept. This can, and does, lead to disillusionment, depression or even withdrawn behaviour from which recovery is neither simple nor easy. In the meantime, we are left with three suffering parties – the teacher, his pupils, and his colleagues. The major factor causing stress appears to be varied forms of breakdown in communications, for example relations between teachers and children, relations between teachers and parents, relations between teachers and teachers and relations between head teachers and teachers. I could go on in an endless permutation setting out the intricacies that make the school whole, but I feel it will be of more use to expose some factors which cause and spread stress more quickly than any gangrenous growth.

Unsuitable timetabling, working conditions and changes in timetabling (at short notice) will often fill a class teacher with a dismay that is difficult to conceal from children, who do not respond well to unprepared change. Inadequate stock, materials and working conditions will all feed and foster fatigue and lessen any teacher's work output. How often have we watched 'remedial' classes being held in cloakrooms, and oh, pity so many poor music teachers valiantly performing in the hall as parents, children from other classes, visitors and helpers all pass by, destroying attention and the creative atmosphere which has so carefully been built up.

In our own building, a break away from routines and rituals was carefully avoided. Specialist teachers were used throughout the school. There were five of them and this meant half-classes for three-fifths of the day for almost all teachers. In this way, with groups of ten, the class teacher could embark on careful remedial work – so much better than a visiting teacher two days a week, stuck in a corridor somewhere, and from a child's point of view more realistic for his particular needs. All the children, boys and girls, took part in housecraft, music, art and craft, and machinery/woodwork and metalwork. The five specialist teachers liaised carefully with each other so that the learning of a trade was always creative as well as being utilitarian. Children were allowed to choose within each class how they wished to group and in all cases they chose mixed groups of boys and girls except between 10 and 12 years. At this stage, it appeared quite definitely that girls wanted to be just with girls some of the time. By thirteen years, this was never the case. Cookery was as popular with boys as it was with girls and why not? It always astonishes me when I survey the number of courses and classes available to girls for preparation for motherhood. Surely, some preparation is needed for the expectancy of fatherhood and at present, provision and guidance in this field is as rare as the giant panda.

All stock was chosen by the staff themselves, with a young teacher accountable for ordering and usage. In this way, all the staff knew how much money was available and how to balance their needs accordingly. They assessed their priorities and needs well, and the stockroom was open to all. This kind of self-service was never misused and little was wasted. New methods were never adopted unless the staff decided collectively to see them through; adapting methods and attitudes before either equipment or the teaching team are remotely ready for them is asking for stress, resulting in a death-wish in terms of educational committal.

There are other factors causing stress which are less easily negotiable: the weather, for instance. Rainy and windy days were always difficult, it meant that teachers and helpers were often with the children almost all of the day without much of a break. Other more obvious factors can be dealt with by the Department of Education and Science or local education authorities. Many teachers (particularly in urban areas) bring in stress from their own home situation, and stress is shed like pollen. In 80 per cent of these cases, one could say that it is a lack of a proper or reasonable home that is the root cause of it. The situation (as in nursery provision in educational priority areas) is verging on the scandalous. The Greater London Council and some of the London boroughs offer sympathy and are fully aware of this problem but are impotent as regards being able to offer any sizeable provision to meet the need. There is a dire need for community schools in urban areas. How can this need be remedied if teachers have no place to live either within or near that community? As things are, it is impossible for them to live near their schools because property and land has been 'councilised' with no provision recommended for teachers. On present salaries, mortgages are impossible. Consequently, they are forced into the twilight bedsitter areas or 'ghetto' flats; seven may be sharing three large rooms and use of lavatory and bath on the landing. Rents for such places are, of course, outrageous, but a teacher's present salary does not give him or her the option of house purchase.

Little wonder then that head teachers feel like teacher social workers; little wonder at the extent of staff turnover in some city schools (as extreme as 100 per cent within a year) when the prospect of such a basic security as adequate living accommodation is so remote for so many of our colleagues. Housing provision for teachers in urban areas is of the utmost necessity. If this is not met, then stability of children and education standards in schools must take a nose-dive, resulting in further increases in delinquency, truancy and all the other allied forms of social malaise that poor schooling helps to engender.

Fortunately, our staff turnover was slender and in times of stress we helped one another. Within the staffroom the clearest sign of a teacher under stress was an overintensity of reaction to a fairly mundane problem or perhaps a laissez-faire attitude to an issue of vital importance. A bland response to stressful behaviour is often more wounding to an adult than a rebuttal, and withdrawn behaviour from a teacher is as serious in its implications as it is from a child.

'He is no problem in school, but I am very worried about him.' This kind of comment from teachers, parents and head teachers would often accompany children like Clarence. He sat there in the chair, expressionless, immobile, seemingly indifferent. Any questions asked were either ignored or answered with a nod or shake of his head. His medical record showed that he had been tested for deafness and that his hearing was perfect. Physically this young West Indian boy looked a very healthy twelve-year-old. His posture, sitting or standing, was as taut as a violin string.

'He speak at home sometime – sometime he shout,' said the mother.

There didn't seem much point in questioning the boy further. It was clear to me that school for him was a bewildering and terrifying place and I did not wish to exacerbate this feeling.

I placed him in Darryl Joyce's class. This young effervescent Australian teacher was bubbling over with ideas but they never spilled out in front of the children with whom he maintained a careful friendly relationship.

'Clarence is working quite hard, but always on his own, Tom. I can't get him to go into any room except mine. He won't go to music, art, craft, housecraft, nothing. He's with me all day, you know how hot this heating gets, well he never even takes his bloody coat off. Even at dinner he sits next to me, ploughs through his meal, then back to the classroom.'

'Are you pushing him?' I asked.

'No, I thought I'd leave it for a bit.'

'Good. I think you're right – at least he's coming into school every day.'

'Yes, but he's not spoken to me yet; it's five weeks you know. He does talk to Derek and sometimes Billy and he likes Christine because he told Derek.'

This evidence of the bush telegraph system operating in East London made me smile.

Clarence did eventually talk to his teacher. It began this way. Derek spoke to Darryl Joyce whilst he was looking at his work.

'Clarence told me to tell you that you were a silly fool.'

'Oh, did he. Well tell him the same from me, and I'd like to hear him read when he's ready.'

Three weeks later Darryl rushed into the staffroom as though he had won the pools.

'He spoke to me today, he marched to my desk, pushed a book in front of me and said, "I can read." He's a good reader and his voice is so deep it's like listening to Paul Robeson. I let him go on for at least ten minutes, then he just said, "I'll finish now," and he did.'

It was clear that Clarence's cautious emergence from his shell had meant as much to his teacher as it had to him.

For months, Clarence continued to exclude himself from the company of the other teachers, but he did begin to acknowledge smiles or a nod of greeting. An enormous mural of the school building was being assembled and every child in the school drew himself and stuck his self-image upon it. Clarence placed his image discreetly behind the rabbit hutches, indicating that he considered he was with us but observing. For some reason there was a helicopter flying over his head. Three weeks later, Clarence left his classroom and took part in a specialist subject. He chose to go to cookery. Here he conformed more, in that he removed his coat and donned an apron. He did not choose to go to art or craft, woodwork or metalwork – I couldn't quite understand why. The answer came unexpectedly, as so often happens in teaching.

I was admiring a huge historical scrapbook on transport that a group of children in Darryl Joyce's class had recently completed. Darryl spoke to me in an undertone.

'Look at Clarence,' he muttered.

'Where is he?' I whispered, as he was nowhere to be seen in the classroom.

'Over in the cookery-room, you can see right in here through the French windows.'

Clarence was busily stirring some mixture. He cracked an egg and tipped it in the bowl with French cuisine *éclat*. At intervals of five minutes or so, he would look across into the classroom and then continue with his scones or cakes.

'It's always the same,' said Darryl. 'Sometimes I smile and he smiles back, and sometimes he doesn't.'

I know now why Clarence had chosen the cookery-room – it was perfectly placed for him to view one of his few security symbols and know that it was not going to disappear.

After a year had passed, Clarence was joining in all aspects of the school day, attending specialist subjects as well as physical education and games. However, sporadically we were subjected to fits of violent and sustained temper when he would attack physically a boy or girl, regardless of his victim's size. These moods of anger and repressed vindictiveness he could sustain for a whole morning or an afternoon and at such times (for the safety of children and staff) he stayed with me in my room. Usually, I tried to divert him into another situation and discuss the matter later and try to rationalise it. Child guidance was suggested but refused, so there were few resources that we could use but our own.

The majority of the staff were against the idea of excluding Clarence from school, but there were a minority who felt his presence placed other children at risk. The minority were probably right, but we didn't exclude him. He did spend two weeks at home after a particularly nasty incident.

He had begun to join in playing football with the other boys on Wednesday afternoon. As far as skill was concerned, he was quite good, but he always played with such fierce intensity that somehow it seemed more of an endurance test than a relaxation. Apart from the physical exercise provided, there could be little fun in it for him, yet he managed for about three months, until one afternoon the door of my room crashed open. It banged against the cupboard, upsetting a totem pole that had been made out of empty paint tins. Two feathers which were stuck on the top fluttered on to the carpet near my feet. I didn't have much time to be amused at this bit of casual pagan destruction. Paul, the games teacher, stood at the doorway, looking shocked and shaken.

'It's Clarence, I've asked him to come . . .'

At this point, Clarence appeared. His face showed no emotion, but he seemed to be staring at something in the distance, not unlike the stare of a blind child. In his right hand he held a broken milk bottle. Paul spoke again.

It's all over an argument with Desmond, you can see what a pitch it's all got to. I think it began yesterday and it's carried over on to the football field.'

I spoke quickly, 'Is Desmond all right?'

'Oh yes, the others are playing again now.'

'Good, I'll stay with Clarence now, you finish the games off and see Desmond home tonight. Close Rosemary's door for me, would you Paul?'

'Yes, will you be OK?'

'I hope so.'

During all this time, Clarence had not moved from the doorway. I didn't much like the look of the jagged milk bottle, but if he had really wanted to use it, I reasoned that he probably would already have done so. All the time I was rationalising with myself in this way, more than likely in order to allay my own fears in the situation. Looking at Clarence, a paternal chat wouldn't have been much use. I decided that if there was to be any physical injury, the best thing to do would be to restrict the numbers of injured.

I took some papers to the filing cabinet, and half turned and gestured with my right hand for Clarence to sit down inside my room. He moved into my room, but did not sit. I pushed the filing cabinet shut, walked over to the door and closed it behind him. He still stood there like Oedipus, pointing the bottle as though it were a walking stick. His grievance or worry was heavy and I knew that it was not based on this solitary incident, but on years of repression. He had got himself to my room, he knew he was in a mess. I wondered what he wanted me to do.

'You'd better not come near me.'

I looked at him and nodded (thank God, he'd started to talk). I turned my back on him (possibly a calculated risk, I can't tell now) and sat at the side of my desk, not behind it. Those huge 'head teacher' desks are often impenetrable physical barriers – or escape routes – there didn't seem much point in placing him farther away from me. He walked towards me slowly, quite deliberately and stopped about a yard away. I remained sitting, but attentive; a lack of concern could have provoked him.

'Are you scared?' he asked.

'Yes, I am, wouldn't you be if you were me?'

'You'd better not try and grab this' – he shook the bottle.

'I am scared Clarence, but I'm puzzled as well, have I had any quarrel with you? Have I said or done anything to upset you? Let me know if I have.'

He shook his head.

'Do you want to hurt me with that thing?'

He shook his head again.

'I'll believe you when you put it in the wastepaper basket, or I'll put it in there for you if you like. Then you can tell me all about it.'

There was a long pause, it must have been seconds but seemed more like hours. I wanted to pull the curtains across the window as the sun was blurring my eyes. It seemed odd that during this kind of tension one could be aware of such minor discomfiture. Clarence broke my reverie: he leaned forward and placed the broken bottle on the splodged blotting paper near the corner of my desk. He sat down and simultaneously I picked up the bottle and dropped it into the wastepaper bin. Tears were beginning to trickle down Clarence's cheeks, but no sound came from him. His anguish was void of sob or sniffle, it was silent and deep.

The words came out in a non-stop torrent of abuse and bitterness; no adjectives were spared. This verbal assault I didn't interrupt, it was better than a physical attack. Concluding his tirade, Clarence clenched his fists and ground his teeth.

'I'm going to get that Desmond and I'm going to kill him. Yes, I'm going to kill him dead.'

It was time for evening assembly. I didn't want to leave Clarence alone – he might attempt to carry out his threats and there was no doubt that this aggressor was suffering. He accompanied me to assembly, without questioning my suggestion. I had hoped that the interval might cool his feelings, but immediately after assembly, he reiterated his intentions. I was in no position to disbelieve him, the risk would have been too great. I stated my position to him.

'You see, Clarence, we would have to stop you doing such a thing and until I feel sure that you won't do it, then you will have to stay out of school for a time.'

'I will do it.'

'Well I'll come home with you tonight and explain the situation to your Dad, you'll just have to stay at home until you feel different. Do you mind me seeing your Dad about it?'

'No.'

I think at this point, Clarence realised that what I proposed to do constituted as much protection for him as it did for Desmond.

Clarence's father greeted me in his pyjamas (I think he was working on a night shift). I explained the situation to him and he listened to it all as though I were explaining fly-fishing. There appeared to be no worry or agitation, he was angry neither with me nor Clarence – Clarence might have been a piece of furniture. He was not referred to in any way at all. I left, saying to Clarence that I was sorry and that I hoped to see him again at school soon and the last view of his father's face was obscured by a yawn.

Clarence returned two weeks later. We were all edgy in case another violent or pseudo-violent outburst might erupt again, but our fears were unfounded and he even talked occasionally to Desmond. However, other children had taken stock of the last occurrence and gave Clarence little or no provocation. He became quietly co-operative, but the terms of his co-operation were almost always engineered by him, so that outwardly we witnessed a boy who seemed to be declaring only a small part of himself; it was the undeclared side which kept us ever watchful. Nevertheless, he became much more sociable and affable and took great delight in joking and quipping and we felt that this newfound sense of humour would improve the prospects of his total development even more. I would like to give a complete happy ending, but cannot. Circumstances made the ending a question mark. There was a breakdown in the parental situation and Clarence had to leave us for boarding school in the countryside. During his holidays he visits us still, but his face and smile remain as enigmatic as the Mona Lisa's and I will never forget his father's yawn.

The numbers of children like Clarence are increasing day by day and all parents and teachers need to be wary of children who apparently present no difficulty whatsoever. If anyone accepts into his home or class a child who makes little demand, presents no obvious troublesome behaviour and shows next to no sense of wonder, then he has good reason to feel uneasy. Other children like Clarence are easily recognised by their self-imposed isolation and this isolation or preoccupation is extended to adults and children alike. It is at the infant stage that this is most pronounced, and it's of no use saying – 'Well, he's no trouble . . .' – he may be later on, and serious trouble at that. Withdrawn behaviour of this nature some-times (as in Clarence's case) explodes into a violent temper tantrum which when first witnessed causes surprise. I can't think why one should be surprised. The water will not simmer for ever.

The children in the school who could have been termed, for one reason or another, part of this group, numbered fifteen. They all seemed to have some or all of the following behaviour patterns. They tended to keep to the sides of the classroom and avoid the centre. Most of them were reluctant to remove their coats. They either over-ate or under-ate, they ate either far more rapidly or far more slowly than normal. All appeared indifferent at work or play. These children would often embark on solitary play in a manner which seemed to dismiss all sense of personal achievement and excitement. To all intents and purposes, they looked like pieces of machinery going through a series of unproductive exercises. Yet, it would have been disastrous for us to conclude that these children were without feelings.

Here are children who initially want to be ignored or for-gotten. In doing this, they can opt out painlessly for a time but the withdrawal is to their own cost if it is accepted. There must be many such children throughout the country and parents and teachers, in trying to help them, may find that 'come-back' is slender. There may be a temptation, coupled with various other classroom or home pressures, to leave such children to 'get on with it'. This temptation needs to be resisted and the utmost in consistent sympathy must be offered. If notice is taken of them every day and in some quiet way their existence is appreciated, this shows that someone cares about them. In this manner, something greater than can be imagined may be achieved. The achievement may not be the teacher's to survey when that child reaches adolescence or adult life, but assuredly it will far outweigh the value of his or her 'O' levels.

5

A MIXED MENU

The most successful and rewarding of all meal-time sessions came about when the kitchen was producing no cooked meals at all. The drivers responsible for the delivery of food were on strike, all of the school stayed with us throughout the day and there were two options open, either the school closed at mid-day or we made some kind of alternative provision. The apparently simple solution of sending out a note asking that children should bring their own food was not at all simple in practice. Our meals had until now been prepared on the premises by a most able and, probably more important, sensitive cook. Mary Bence was nearing retirement when she came to us; however, she was usually at school at dawn sorting out intricacies of preparation which, on a tight budget, could produce an attractive and appetising weekly menu. I never heard any child complain about the meals and children can be harsh critics as far as food is concerned. True worth is not known until it has gone and now, through no fault of our own, we had temporarily lost our cook. We had no time to be self-indulgent about our loss: many of our families would have collapsed financially if both parents were not working and some children were of one-parent families. A letter was eventually sent to all parents asking them to provide what they could for a mid-day meal. If any parents were free during meal-time periods, they were asked if they would like to come along and assist us with feeding smaller children. Meals until the strike was settled were to be eaten in classrooms. After this we could only wait to see what fate would bring on the following Monday.

'Tom, I'm very worried – Susan Hinton has only brought a bag of crisps for her lunch. I've put all the food in their lockers. Mrs Kingsley says she didn't get on the coach with anything more. Ruth Cohen has enough sandwiches with her to sink a battleship and she's supposed to be on a diet.'

Each class teacher reported almost the same story. There was little we could do on that first day, but wait. If the world could act as our children did then, there would be no underdeveloped or underfed countries today. As teachers, we had no legal right to coerce the children into sharing their food, but food was shared without fuss or ceremony and children who had more than enough gave to children who had little without adult prompting. In fact, there was an overall surplus of food in some classes, so no child went short.

A few mothers answered our appeals for help.

'Oh, hello, Mr Wakefield, I glad to see you. I can't stay long, I have to get back to work for one o'clock but my governor say I can make the half-hour up tonight, so I can stay here till quarter past. Denton gettin' on so well with his readin' now, I very pleased with him and he make me laugh so. He say the class make jelly yesterday to eat today, but he not like the flavour they make. Oh, can I put this down here a minute it burn my fingers?'

Mrs Duckworth laughed loud and long as she placed an enormous towel-covered offering on my desk. Clouds of steam began to fill the office and my secretary's perfume was obliterated by a strong smell of spiced fish.

'I make enough for his teacher also,' said Mrs Denton. She proudly peeled the towels away to reveal a hot fish casserole. 'Can I take it along now, because I must rush to get back to work.'

'Yes do, but what about your own lunch?'

'Oh I eat tonight, don't worry.'

Every day of the strike, Mrs Duckworth delivered her cooked goods as well as working all day to support her family. She always came in smiling, moving and talking quickly. She wore black slacks and a multi-coloured blouse and perched jauntily on her head was a purple crocheted beret. I don't know whether it was her dress or the swiftness or directness of her manner – but I always had the distinct feeling that she was a female jockey. I told her so once and she proceeded to gallop out of the building laughing and smiling more than when she had come in. No people on earth can cook fish like St Lucians and a St Lucian smile is even more expansive and embracing than a Jamaican one. Jewish parents were, as always, most generous, usually sending extra food with a note:

Dear Mr Wakefield,

David has his lunch in the brown parcel, will you please see that he eats his salmon, it is in the plastic wrapper. I have put some cakes and fruit in the carrier bag and these are for the class or who you might think would want them. Thank you for your kindness and could you tell Mrs Harding I have got an iron for her at cost price. She asked me to get one.

Yours faithfully,
I. Levy

PS I do not want David to go swimming this week, he has a bad cold.

The strike lasted for a week or so and this Jamaican letter suitably bids the situation farewell.

Hello Teacher,

Thank you so much for taking Maralyn to the dancing theater, she likes it very much. I am giving her one week and two days over dinner money. I am glad meal-times is regular now. Maralyn told me about the jelly and fruit. My foot is better now, but I must not put the heel on the floor, the doctor say so. You have a good rest in the holiday soon. Thank you teacher.

We had supplemented our make-do meal-service from our own school fund. This fund we raised ourselves and used when and how we thought fit; there was always a need and since the money was never in the bank long enough to earn any interest we had to raise every penny ourselves. Our major sources of income were jumble sales. We held these twice each year. The staff approached their onset as one contemplates a ride on the big dipper – a certain amount of dread mixed with some excitement and thrills, the latter ingredients usually being retrospective rather than immediate. There was not much jumble to be had from our own families; 'hand-me-downs' were rarely thrown out as there was usually a younger child to pass them on to. The staff brought in great bundles from their own neighbours and friends and my secretary's ingenuity in finding firms, factories and shops with obsolete stock knew no bounds. For the two months preceding each sale, the school was a storehouse of clothing, bric-à-brac, wallpapers and paints, house plants and anything saleable from a vacuum cleaner to an overdressed doll which walked and talked and wet its knickers.

A small advertisement in the local paper coupled with our own notices displayed outside the school guaranteed a capacity attendance. The sale was due to commence at 6.30 pm, but long queues would begin to form from 3.00 pm onwards, even before the ordinary school working day had finished. The first fifteen or so in the queue were totters. These are jumble sale professionals who often buy and re-sell at a profit. They were armed with bags hanging over both arms – bags which, when filled, could have stocked a draper's shop. Their capacity seemed limitless and their owners, on leaving the building, resembled refugees who carried their total possessions like human camels or pack-horses. Herbert stood in readiness at the door to receive the small entrance fee. None passed him without payment except for children and the elderly, whom he let in free. Teachers, parents and older children took their places behind the counters which were arranged in the fashion of a 'wagon-square' drawn up against a Red Indian attack. The doors were opened precisely on time and within ten minutes battle commenced.

One elderly lady who had been given precedence in the queue on account of her partial blindness seemed to have her sight restored as she descended the steps and entered the hall. Her white stick was flung over her shoulder in rifle fashion and she managed to select her purchases without help, in spite of her affliction. Others in the queue did direct some abuse at her, but there was no time for quarrelling. The last I saw of her she was pushing a woollen dress into an enormous plastic bag and shouting at one of the crowd who had questioned her integrity.

'I've got me book to prove it, so save yer bleedin' breath.'

The first detachment of buyers were always the shrewdest bargainers. My secretary was immune to the onslaughts.

'It's five pence, dear.'

'I'll give three for it.'

'No, it's worth twenty and I'm letting it go for five.'

'Look, give me these pyjamas as well and we'll call it a deal, OK?'

'No, it's five pence or no deal.'

'Keep it then . . . Oh, you've not sold it to her now. I was goin' to buy it. Now you've sold it to her, you're no judge of character. I've known her since she was a young married woman, she took in washin' then. Oh, you never gave her your washin' to do of a Friday cos' she'd pawn it over the weekend. You couldn't get it back till the next Wednesday, that's what she's like and you sold her the coat. Oh, you're hard you are, I can see it in your face.'

By this time, my secretary had turned to the next customer

and the lady who was questioning her compassion stole the children's pyjamas, swiftly pushing them into the depths of her blue plastic bag. A sixth of our merchandise must have disappeared in this way, but we regarded it as an occupational hazard.

As I handed out a roll of wallpaper, someone tapped my shoulder. I didn't look round.

'You can get change in the office.'

'It's me, Pauline, I don't want change, I've come to help. I'm sorry I couldn't get no sooner, but the chemist's that I work for don't close until six o'clock and I had to wait for a bus.'

I stopped selling and looked round. Pauline had been referred to us from a comprehensive school, she was depressed and withdrawn on arrival, but left us far more confident, but still rather shy.

'I saw your advert in the paper – a lot of the same teachers are here aren't they? I'll go and help Mr Baker on shoes, that's the hardest stall, because you can't get one to match another one and people keep mixing them up.'

I was very pleased to see her and she knew it.

'Are you enjoying your job?'

She smiled, 'Yes, but my feet ache sometimes.'

'It's good of you to come along and help us. You're looking very attractive, Pauline.'

She retorted quickly, 'So's Mr Baker – I'll go and give him a hand, see you Sir.'

For two seconds it was my turn to smile before the next customer broke my reverie with a request for a dented tin of paint. Selling was intense and hectic but never slow, pauses were taken, raffle ticket winnings claimed, baskets of fruit, or cakes, or rehabilitated vacuum cleaners. After two hours the selling declined rapidly and our older girls did a brisk trade selling cakes they had made in school. Tea flowed on and on until the last customers trailed out with their bags bulging, well-pleased with bargains that had meant so little to someone else. From this particular sale, we earned a hundred and fifty pounds. The helpers, teachers, parents, pupils and ex-pupils did not stop working. They immediately began clearing-up operations, their fatigue vanishing as they cleared away remnants of clothing, shattered books and chipped or cracked ornaments that had not been able to find a home. There was a drink of home-made wine in the staffroom and when the hall was clear I could hear teachers and parents recounting anecdotes of the evening and chuckling over the splendid chaos of the sale.

I looked round the hall, checking that all was prepared for the next working school day. No vestige of the busy evening was left except for a solitary shoe. It was a lady's shoe, probably dating from the early fifties. I turned it over in my hands. It was a shiny pink patent leather object that had lost its former lustre. Flakes of leather had fallen from it and one of the glittering buttons was lost. It was very narrow, with a spindly heel and a toe which ended in a spear-point. Its shape must have represented dancehall agony for the wearer similar to Chinese foot-binding. One felt that it was almost a museum-piece, bringing to mind the ballroom with the great revolving mirror turning round for the inevitable spot-waltz, excuse-me tango or the interruption quickstep. Looking at the shoe, I couldn't help thinking of the mother who had sent it in. I wondered if she had time to consider it with nostalgia or regret – she probably didn't. I dropped it into the rubbish bag and joined the others in the staffroom. I hope jumble sales will always be called jumble sales, not 'summer fairs' or 'selling fetes' – the new nomenclatures seem to destroy the pink pointed shoe and that's a great pity.

Jumble sales and lunch-times might seem odd times for sharpening observation and insight, but the idlest gleaner could gather something from such times. Memories of certain conversations have not dimmed with the passing of time.

'Oh, Nigel, you've made Tina cry. I thought you liked her.'

'I do like her. I don't want to make her cry.'

'Well you have, she says you've flicked a piece of carrot on to her plate off the table and spoiled her jam roll.'

'I just flicked it like this, not at her, it just fell there.'

'Would you like to get her another pudding or give her some of yours?'

'I'll get her some more.'

Tina had stopped crying by now and Nigel returned with the unsullied jam roll and custard.

'You sit with Tina now. You wouldn't like your pudding spoiled would you? No. Neither does anyone else here, so don't flick your food.'

'All right.'

Meal-times were initially very hard. The staff had chosen to eat with the children and all of us, adults, adolescents, primaries and infants sat together at one sitting. At first we were all subjected to variations on the kind of dialogue I have just reproduced. It might be funny to read, but after a morning's teaching, such incidents could be most wearing. Soon the situation improved and our eating-times together often proved to be the most relaxing and rewarding parts of the day. I would never have dreamed that so many troubles and tensions could have been ironed out via apple pie and sausage and mash. It was a time, too, when older children could help younger ones.

'Oh, Beverley, that is good of you to help Peter like that. Have you got any custard on your shirt?'

'No, it OK. He very naughty. I not know how Mrs Krever stand him.'

'He'll get better, soon he'll be as helpful as you are.'

'I'll clean him up a bit, can I use the medical room? Peter, your Mummy be very angry with you if she know you tip up your . . .'

Conversation with withdrawn children was also easier at meal-times. The passing of the salt and pepper to such children by a friendly adult constituted much more than an introduction to the second course.

Our children found free play periods difficult and there were often quarrels and fights. Anguish was the key-note rather than laughter. Slides, climbing frames, adventure materials were provided but they did not solve the endless difficulties. I had also noticed how badly the children recovered from break periods and anxieties from break often overlapped into the building and classrooms long afterwards. For these reasons, we decided to escort our children out to play and also meet them, greet them and bring them back in again. The number of adults on duty in the playground was increased to five each period: one teacher, two mothers and two helpers. It worked. The mothers played with the children, introducing long-lost collective street games that they had remembered from childhood. Slowly but surely fights and quarrels decreased and break-times were no longer sources of trepidation for children or teachers. We continued to escort children in and out of school. This did not imply rigid formal lines of children waiting for a roll-call. It represented a friendly escort who contributed stability to children who were asking for it in the only way they knew how.

In the same way, children were sent home in the evening after a short assembly in which we said goodnight. At times, this period was used for additional commendations and praise. Quite spontaneously, smaller children would kiss class teachers before leaving. I can remember one important lady visitor in a huge green hat who had her lipstick ruined by infant ardour. She didn't seem to mind. Older children were never embarrassed by these demonstrations of affection and the more I view the all-age school, the more I realise the cruelty of segregating children by age. The loss in terms of total development and stabilisation must be enormous.

In games the school did well. West Indians in this quarter, as in music, gave a great deal. Their zest and enthusiasm knew no bounds. Neither, in a sense, did their emotions. When they were sad, they were very sad, but when they were happy, everybody was happy. Of the immigrant section within the school, the West Indians presented the largest single group. It had been suggested by many educationists that these children were with us because of 'language development' problems. Nothing could have been farther from the truth. If anything, their language and verbal expression was their greatest asset and we built on this; only two were even aware of the existence of West Indian 'patois' and neither of these used it. They had differing accents, but these were no more of a school handicap than any working-class child had in the Black Country, Norfolk or Gateshead. However, it was singularly apparent that they did, as far as social background were concerned, constitute the 'new poor', and they were afflicted with all the educational ills which attend such poverty. The basic factors in most cases for placement were definitely social and not genetic.

Up to fifteen children each year were transferred back to ordinary schools. Parents were often apprehensive about this; they had seen their children improve and they knew that if they stayed with us we would find them work and continue to take an interest in them beyond school. They knew that we maintained an umbilical relationship with the children from fourteen upwards in that they attended the local technical college for two or three days each week and spent the rest of the time with us. It was a difficult decision to make and I let the parents make it. I always insisted that they visit the school that their child was transferring to, just to see if they liked it. This was not always the case and here I always advised them firmly on their parental rights.

Dear Mr Wakefield,
    I thankyou for geting me to my new big school. I did not want to go at first but now I want to go and I will be starting on Monday the 26th of March and I cannot wait to start the

new school and I have a friend going to that school and she say it is a great school I hope she right because I like your school. I like the teachers, they been good and kind to and teach me everything they no. And when I came to your school I did not know how to read or spell. I miss Mrs Gates and Miss Pope.
The End.
TO MR WAKEFIELD

Dear Mr Wakefield,
I went to thank you for geting me into my new big school and I no that I am going to like it very much because the next school I was going to I had a lot of friends and a lot off them went to this school. Four a long time we did not see each other but very soon we are going to be together again and I thank you four everything you did and when I first came to your school I did not like it a bit but as the weeks past I got to like it and then I got to like games that we do and net-ball and going swimming and dancing in the Hall. I like going running and I like everything we do in your school and I like this school very much and I wish I did not have to leave, but I want to go now and I won't fourget this school. And I won't fourget the teacher and all the teacher was very kind to me and I won't fourget that, and I was very horrible to them sometimes, and I like Miss Pope very much and I went to thank all teacher who did have me in class four and class five and those teachers teach me evertings I no. But I don't want to live them but I moss go and I went to say good-bye everybody and hope to see everybody again and I want to thank all the cook four lovely dinner we had in this school and Miss reid for her cookery.

Eighty per cent of the transfers were successful; the failures were usually withdrawn children whom we had felt had become sufficiently confident to manage a large school. Particularly, I remember Donna and Deborah – looking at them when they were due to start at their new comprehensive school, all scrubbed and fresh in their new bottle-green uniforms. After two months had passed, I remember both their mothers coming to me in desperation, pleading for me to take them back. They had no need to plead. One look at their daughters told me all that I needed to know. They looked white, pinched and drawn, their long hair covered eyes that were dark with strain and unhappiness. They were both truanting and had absented themselves with one illness after another for their last three weeks in school. I don't think those illnesses were feigned. I took them back.

6

THREE GIRLS AND A GREEN PLASTIC MAC

Immigrants quietly rejected stories that were part of their 'cultural heritage'. Visitors would often look at the array of *West Indian Folk Stories* and *Hindu Fables* that I had thought would be of fascination to the children.

'Oh, I've read this collection, I think they are delightful, don't you?' asked an interested and kindly visitor.

'Yes, I do like them.'

I only wished that the children had shared our enthusiasms, but this was not the case. They were city children now and bamboo leaves, palm trees and yam yams meant nothing to them.

Stories were always told and not read.

'Oh sir, we don't want to hear about that stuff,' said Shirley, with adolescent honesty. 'Tell us the story about the pear tree again. You know th ; one where that couple buy a house and they have two kids and a lovely tree in the garden – do you remember? Then the lady sees her husband kissin' another girl and she don't like the tree in the garden any more and leaves him.'

'She didn't leave him,' said Melva.

'No they made up again.'

'She stayed with him because of the kids.'

'He like his wife most really, anyway. She weren't goin' to leave the house.'

These girls were talking about an adaptation of 'Bliss' by Katherine Mansfield, which had enthralled them.

Traditional fairy stories were always popular, which is hardly surprising. These stories are not only the product of imagination, but also its stimulus. In most fairy stories the heroes or heroines are just human beings, after all, but they are usually surrounded by an atmosphere of fulfilled wishes and magic. Fortunately the heroes and heroines are usually of marriageable age except where children are concerned and, for good measure, hero and heroine usually have entirely different social backgrounds, Royalty marries the beggar; and Herbert had already proved (like others before him) that the son of a carpenter could be a king.

Story-telling did provide a major form of communication as well as a stimulus for imagination which extended to all subjects. Most teachers preferred stories placed at the end of the day, giving the following reasons for this:

1 Less likelihood of interruption, which was true. Children hate having stories interrupted by visitors, medicals or grouping in timetabling.
2 Many teachers felt that it was a calming influence on the children before leaving school for home. In this respect it might be as well to recognise that the teacher also was 'closing' the day relatively quietly.
3 Comprehension or understanding seemed better after the story had been 'digested'. It was often an excellent opening for an English activity period the next day.

A story can be integrated into the timetable creatively in numerous ways. I believe it can stand in its entirety without any follow-up whatsoever. Just as a child may look at a picture and say 'Oh, it's lovely, Miss' or 'Oh, Sir, was it really like that?', so in the same way he can express his feelings about the story which is told just for its telling. Intense verbal dissection of a story eventually disintegrates into the verbal questioning diatribe that kills a story. Disturbed and backward children seem to find prolonged question and answer sessions annoying and in consequence become irritable.

'What was the name of the old woman?'

'Yes, and where did she live?'

'What was growing in her garden?'

'Do you think her son was . . . ?'

A total analysis of the story in this way is rather destructive as far as the use of imaginative resources are concerned. Comprehension by acting proved much more favourable and improvisations in the classroom were always the most vital and illuminating forms of recapitulation. Telling a story also seemed to be the simplest and most informative way of giving our children some historical and geographical background. With very young children it was possible to give them some identification with the characters in the story whilst at the same time making the environment different.

'Jennifer had black curly hair, and very large dark brown eyes, her skin was the colour of chocolate and she loved skipping – just like you do Janet. But she didn't live in a high block of flats. Oh no, she lived in a small house (it only had one room and a kitchen) with her old grandmother. On the floor of the house there were beautiful rugs of many different colours. Her grandmother spent most of the time making rugs which she sold in the market place. Sometimes Jennifer would go with her granny to the market place. It was very busy there, lots of people were selling all kinds of things there. And from her granny's tiny market stall, Jennifer could see the big blue sea.'

In this way it was possible to present a natural and unforced introduction to a preliminary study of the West Indies. Social history and working conditions were dealt with similarly. Stories of fortitude and courage with a historical background were popular with all age groups and even at a very early age children realised that the finest heroic achievements were not necessarily limited to the battlefield. These stories often led to creative work in other areas like art, music and craft. Cardboard models and masks of giants festooned the building and through children's fingers the building was invested with its own imagination and magic.

The simplest working materials were the most satisfactory with disturbed children. It was also important that the model-making activity didn't last too long. Young disturbed children tended to want to see the finished model quickly. They wanted to achieve satisfaction and success without too much stress. Plasticine, papier mâché, clay and balsa wood can translate into form quickly and thus boredom was avoided. Some of the withdrawn approached the use of clay with great reluctance. It seemed the best way to introduce them to the feel and touch of clay was by letting them play with water first. Just consider the usefulness of a plastic cosmetic or detergent bottle when placed in a bath. It can float, squirt, fill and empty, go up and down like a submarine or a diver and is often much more of a constant source of information and delight to a young child than any expensive toy.

The stories also led to dramatic play and improvisation and with young disturbed children, many of whom were at the 'nursery stage' of maturity, it took on critical importance in both social development and mental health. This kind of play did soothe some of the frustrations of their everyday life and helped them accept the world as it was more easily.

Puppetry was a boon to many of the withdrawn children. Voices that had only been known to whisper or squeak were transformed by the gloved hands and the cloth screen. For once in their lives they began to use imperative gestures and verbal commands.

'You mean to tell me that all you've got for our brown and white cow is beans?'

'Yes.'

'Beans, beans, what's the use of beans? It's money I needed

you stupid boy. These beans are useless. There.' (Throws the beans out of the window.)

The gloved hand showed no temerity as it shook and walloped poor Jack. It was difficult to remember that behind the screen the young puppeteer was a timid, shy, inadequate little girl.

The children that we could not help were children who were literally taken from us. Selina and Marina Harrington were sisters who both found their way to us. Selina's entrance was more rapid as she had been excluded from infants school at six and a half years of age. This is not to say that the particular school had not tried with her – but, according to the school and all medical reports, her condition had so deteriorated that they were no longer able to cope. They had witnessed a non-co-operative little girl who spent most of the day indulging in fierce temper tantrums. In a very lame frame of mind I looked at the IQ test – 52; after that I dismissed it from my mind, not cynically, just with a sense of sadness that they had even bothered with the expense of testing.

Of the temper tantrums we were left in no doubt. In the first three weeks of Selina's school life with us, she averaged nine each day and one day she hit the all-time record of fifteen. They would usually take the form of a boiling rage, instigated or provoked by a situation which she herself had arranged. For seemingly no reason, jig-saw pieces would suddenly be scattered on the floor, followed by foot-stamping, spitting, screaming and tears. In the midst of all this, she would choose to hurt herself rather than other children, banging herself on desks or knocking herself on cupboards and adding to her self-induced distress.

Brenda Harding would try to divert her and at times the screams and crying would reduce Selina to a bedraggled, exhausted little girl who accepted comfort and cosseting more out of fatigue and numbness than anything else. At times the situation was so critical that she had to remain with me in my room – havoc was created. The telephone was knocked across the desk, toys slung at the wall, she would throw herself on to the floor and yell abuse. In spite of all this, through all her distraction, an objective onlooker could not fail to see a very pretty little girl. The squinting and tension hid large light blue eyes and the fine blonde hair, always in matted disarray, framed a pert little face.

We built on this: 'Oh, Selina, you do look pretty today— doesn't she Mrs Harding?'

'Yes, and she has a secret that she hasn't let you know about.'

'Oh, can Mrs Harding tell me your secret, Selina?'

Brenda whispers to Selina. Selina nods her head in answer to the teacher-child confidentiality.

'Well, she sings beautifully and she sang to all of us today.'

Selina managed a broken smile as other infants raised their voices in an affirmative chorus. A few weeks later Selina sang for us in assembly and was enraptured with her ovation. Gradually the tempers grew less in number and her work progressed as one would have expected it to.

Work with Selina could not end in school; her teacher sought out Mrs Harrington at home and they became friends. She babysat, talked, laughed and got Mrs Harrington to visit the school – there was no Mr Harrington and, with two small children, she was forced to manage on social security. Both her children were attending special schools, and it was Mrs Harrington herself who informed me that Marina was also to join us.

'I'm glad Marina is coming 'ere, there's nothin' wrong with her legs or anythin' like that.'

My puzzled expression must have posed my question. I didn't have to speak. She continued,

'Yes, the doctors said she could come here and as Selina is comin' on so well, I was glad about it to tell you the truth. She shouldn't really be with all those cripples.'

'Well, I haven't heard anything about it yet, but I'll let you know as soon as I do.'

'Oh, you'll hear, they told me last week.'

She was quite right, the papers arrived four days later. Marina had been admitted to a school for physically handi-capped children with a very questionable prognosis of minimal brain damage. She was awkward and tense and subject to some temper tantrums, but they were mild and less frequent than those of her sister. Needless to say, her IQ was well within the statutory range of what is still termed educational sub-normality. The two sisters helped one another and it was good that they were together. After two years, Selina's tempers were rarities and her IQ registered at 91 (average!). Mrs Harrington rejected the idea of ordinary school transfer, possibly because she had come to rely on the school as much as her children did. Selina proved to be a marvellous actress and her improvisations in assemblies and classroom gave her esteem as well as delight.

Yes, we all felt very happy about the Harringtons. Then, just before Christmas, the phone rang.

'Hello, Mr Wakefield, Social Services Department here.'

'Yes?'

'You have two little girls on your roll I believe – Harrington is the name.'

'Yes, Selina and Marina. They are not in school today.'

'I know. They have been taken into care.'

'Which care? Where? What's happened to them?'

'Well, it's rather a long story, I won't go into it on the telephone. They are in Buckinghamshire at the moment. The countryside – High Wycombe in fact.'

'Well get them back.'

'I beg your pardon?'

'I said, could you get them back? Why have they been sent to High Wycombe? Why aren't they in a foster home near us? At least, they would be near someone they know.'

'It is awful, but we had a terrible time even getting them in there. There were just no places available in the borough and this was the best we could do. Can I telephone you later and I'll look into it all a bit more deeply for you?'

I could never bring myself to be bucolic about the country-side and wax effusive about it to city children who were being sent there. Why should they hold a tree in awe and revere a shorn sheep? Why couldn't a roaring petrol lorry and winking traffic lights hold as much fascination – they probably did. We had even adapted songs to the city, one to a well-known hymn tune.

> The buildings tall, the roof-tops high,
> The drifting cranes across the sky
> Oh, I'm as rich, as rich can be
> For all of London belongs to me.

How I longed to own just one old house near the school – some were empty anyway. A short stay hostel could have stopped so many families from splitting in all directions and if the policy-makers wanted to talk economics, this would still be more viable than a boarding school or 'long term care'. In fact, we were trying to buy such a property, but energy as well as money was scarce at the end of most of our working days and after three years we were still at the stage of trying to get enough money for a mortgage. Our intention was to buy the house first and ask questions about staffing later.

The following day gave me an insight into what had crushed the Harrington family. It seemed that Mrs Harrington had been occupied in some activities of which her neighbours did not approve – nothing illegal. The so-called neighbours had kicked doors and smashed windows of the tiny flat. The result of this onslaught shattered what confidence Mrs Harrington had left and the children were panic-stricken. Mrs Harrington was under medical care and the children, after much to-ing and fro-ing to try to find them a local home, were finally shipped out to High Wycombe, which might well have been Siberia as far as their schooling was concerned. I made appealing and angry calls to the Social Services Department, but they could not find a place locally for the little girls. My initial reaction was to blame and attack the system, but the story there was just the same – creaking resources, huge staff turnover and a limit to what anyone could do. Many of the teachers suggested that they could look after the girls in their own homes throughout the holiday period, but we could get no assurance as to when they would come back and a double break might have been even more upsetting for them. A teacher did go to visit them, but I wonder whether this assuaged or increased the girls' anxiety. It was clear that they would miss Christmas with us and by this time, they were as much a loss to us as we were to them. In mid-December the housemother of the hostel where they were staying telephoned. She was a kindly Scots woman.

'Mr Wakefield? I'm phoning about Selina and Marina. I'm most worried about them – I can't find a school for them around here. There are no schools like yours in this area and I'm worried about their education.'

I was worried about far more than their education.

'Contact the Social Services, contact Education Welfare – here are the numbers, tell them what you have told me. Those children should be here in London where they belong.'

'I agree with you, yes, I'll do what you say, it is such a dreadful shame.'

'Oh, you can tell them that the headmaster categorically refuses to take them off his official school roll. Will you do that?'

'Yes, yes, of course, thank you – goodbye.'

Four months has passed and those girls are still, at the time of writing, in High Wycombe: their names on countless forms, reposing on the desks of clerks, social workers and such. In the meantime, all I can think of are the tear-stained faces and the amount of human suffering a little girl of seven and one of eight can absorb.

Brenda Haigh could have stepped from the pages of a history book about the poor of the 1880s. Her clothes were ill-fitting, dirty and torn, her hair was bedraggled and her hands and lips were covered in sores and scratches. She wouldn't look up from the floor when I first met her – but responded warmly to the Irish social worker who accompanied her into school on her first day. Neither of her parents was present. The hemline of her turned-up dress had half-fallen and she looked a very lopsided eleven-year-old. Her cardigan had lost all semblance of colour and two of the five buttons were missing. There was also a distinct smell of stale urine.

The school doctor called at least once a week, sometimes twice. She had worked in the area for many years and knew the families very well. She lived in a London suburb very different from the East End of London where we were placed, but the twenty-mile journey every day did not seem to trouble her. In fact, this kindly, rather shy woman adored most forms of travel; at fifty, she was happy cycling or journeying through South America by train. Trains were her hobby and she enthusiastically shared this interest with her husband. Our medical room was not covered in eye charts or teeth in stages of decay. The children had painted a huge engine for her which sped across the room – a mobile of trucks was suspended from the ceiling and the special therapist always left some homely bits of paraphernalia lying about. The room did not smell of Dettol, and huge sunflowers grew outside the window. Most of the doctor's time was spent in medicals and IQ testing. She herself often stated quite openly that the test couldn't give a very clear guide with many of the children. It was known as a statutory review and before she tested, I always said, 'Look, I'll bet it'll be about . . .' I wasn't guessing so much as making an assumption based on a child's emotional condition. She could verify that I was never far out.

Parents were always consulted and asked if they wished to attend. The majority did not – often both parents were at work. Some children were always curiously absent when a medical had been arranged, usually with parental support.

'Oh, Mr Wakefield, is that you? Mr Mehetma here, Fatima cannot be in today. She has a bad throat, she is sick and her back ache.'

'Oh, I'm sorry, she does sound very ill. Did you contact the doctor?'

'No, I think she will be better tomorrow or the day after.'

Such rapid recoveries were not uncommon at these times; again, there was a deep-rooted suspicion of an official inspection of any kind. The parents who did come enjoyed themselves, sitting there with their tea. I remember Mrs Anderton, one of our school parent governors. A large, warm, lovely West Indian lady, sitting smiling and talking to everyone. 'Hello, my darlings, yes my leg is much better now, my ankle has gone down and the hospital are very pleased with me. Now Miss Pope, don't you kill yourself with work, you gotta look after yourself too. I'm very pleased with David, he don't like seeing the doctor, that's why I come. Al is better if he knows I am just sitting here. Did you like your shave lotion Mr Foster? It make you smell nice – all the ladies like you.'

If children were attending a statutory review, then it was a simple process. I took them along to the medical room.

'You know Dr Fisher, she's a friend of mine, she would like you to do some puzzles, maybe read for her.'

We tried to dispel any tension that the room might hold; but in spite of its looking adventuresome rather than clinical, medicals always caused a certain amount of discomfort. There was always one major fear and it was reiterated by young and older children alike.

'It's not the needle is it? Oh, sir, I don't like it, do I have to have it? It's horrible.'

Apart from polio and TB injections, there were not many. We always remained with the children when they did take place but in spite of the brave show, I am sure that many of them experienced abject terror at such times. Is it too much to hope that oral vaccines may well put the 'needle' out of business in the near future?

Brenda Haigh was due for a medical two days after she arrived. Her parents were absent, but her father had given written permission for it to take place. Present at such medicals were the doctor, a nursing sister, the Education Welfare Officer and, in Brenda's case, a social worker connected with the family. The poor girl was in a sorry state. Her underclothes were dirty and foul with urine, her clothing was inadequate, her shoes worn and downtrodden. Her head was teeming with nits and lice and the scalp was covered in crustaceous scabs where the child had tried to remedy the situation with her nails. In cases of head lice, the following note was supposed to be sent to parents, together with a tube of 'lice-detonator' shampoo.

Dear Parent,

—— was examined today and a few nits were found in his/her hair. The nits can be removed by using the special shampoo as follows:

1 Wet the hair.
2 Rub in about two inches of the shampoo and work well into the scalp.
3 Rinse well with warm water.
4 Apply more shampoo and work well into a good lather.
5 Rinse thoroughly.
6 Comb the hair while wet with a fine tooth comb and then dry.
7 Repeat the treatment about one week later.

The incidence of head lice has recently increased throughout the country and they can spread rapidly from one member of the family to another without any noticeable signs. It is important, therefore, that the entire family should be treated whenever any one member becomes infested. The tube of shampoo contains sufficient for up to six treatments.

If you should need further help, arrangements can be made for treatment at either : . . .

I could never bring myself to send it and always contacted the parents myself. Often they would ask me to arrange the 'detonated' shampoo in school and in some cases, where a child contracted lice regularly, it was much simpler for us to deal with the problem. Such a letter must produce a certain stigma that can often be hurtful. In ordinary schools, when such a letter has been handed out, I've heard 'Oh, she's got fleas, she 'as bugs in 'er head.'

Children have been suspended from school on health grounds for being lousy. I feel this is barbaric as well as a waste of time. With Dad's permission, Brenda was treated at school and she also had a private bath in the tiny flat near the housecraft room, where she luxuriated in talcum powder, bath cubes and bubbles. These feminine niceties coupled with new clothing transformed her, or rather showed her what an attractive girl she was. Her behaviour was very quiet but she was interested and largely co-operative. After a few months there was a dramatic and sudden change in her behaviour. She became sullen, depressed and completely unco-operative. The cause became clear after a home report from Hazel Block. Mrs Haigh had been having psychiatric help, but her relationship with her husband had been strained for some time. Yet she was fond of her four young children and, within her limited resources, tried her best. The situation had finally collapsed: to put it in Brenda's own words, 'My Mum's gone off wiv anuvver man.'

Mr Haigh had his work as well as his family to look after and it seemed that yet another family might be disbanded and taken into care. We were determined that this was not going to happen: telephones rang, voices shouted, cajoled and charmed and finally a home help was arranged for Mr Haigh. This lady visited daily, cleaning, cooking and getting the children off to school. Brenda recovered and, like most crushed plants, improved with the care and attention. Nothing more was heard of Mrs Haigh, but I knew that her husband was desperately trying to trace her. She could not be found. A letter arrived on my desk; the postmark had been obliterated by the rain and there was 2p to pay on delivery, as the sender had not put enough stamps on the envelope.

Dear Sir,
  I ecept you think I'm bad and don't car about the children. It's all lying what they say. I want to tell you abut it. Do not tell the police or enybody, they are all after me. If you want to see me I meet you outside the 106 bus stop near the cemitry at 8 – half-past. DO NOT TELL ANYONE.
Yours sincirly
Mrs Haigh

I respected Mrs Haigh's request for confidentiality and told no one. The day was an arduous one, two teachers had been absent ill and I had taught all the afternoon as well as dealing with a number of minor upsets, including an epileptic fit. This was followed by a meeting of the group who were trying to buy a home/hostel for the school. I left the building at 7.30 pm, had a damp ham sandwich and a cup of tea in a local cafe and made my way to my destination. I arrived at 8.15 – there was no shelter at the bus-stop and it had begun to drizzle. One bus after another sped by as the drizzle turned into heavy rain. I had to keep wiping the rain from my glasses because if Mrs Haigh did arrive, I didn't want to miss her. But what did she look like? How would she arrive? How would she know me? All these questions added to my consternation and the rain and surroundings did nothing to help.

The cemetery was locked: two huge iron gates finalising it all. Through the bars I could see overgrown grave mounds, vaults, desolate crosses, and neglected angels lurching in all directions as though intoxicated with the rain. I walked from the iron gates back to the bus-stop, repeating the process many times in the space of forty minutes.

'Hello.' A woman all in plastic called to me from the other side of the road. I smiled as she picked her way carefully over the slippery zebra crossing. She wore a plastic pixie hood thing on her head, a transparent green plastic raincoat and the final flourish was what looked like plastic envelopes bound over her shoes and tied at the ankles.

'Hello, Mrs Haigh?' I asked.

'Who?'

'Are you Mrs Haigh?'

'No, you bin stood up, you don't want to be standin' round in this weather. It'll kill you. Nobody's worth that much are they?'

'Yes, this one is.'

I didn't want to hurt Miss Plastic's feelings, she seemed nice enough but she had to be removed quickly. She gave me a withering stare, turned and slithered off into the night. I waited until half past ten but no one came. I caught the same 106 bus that I had watched pass by a score of times in the hope of seeing a mother whom I had never met.

Strangely enough, I was not despondent. Afterwards, sitting at home with my cocoa, I felt more than grateful and quite happy that I had received the letter at all. At least the children had not been separated, and Mr Haigh was not managing too badly. I hoped things would work out for Mrs Haigh too, but I'll probably never know. If she does write again, I do know that I shall wait once more, if she asks me to.

7

RESIDENTS AND VISITORS

Parents were, not surprisingly, much more forthcoming when they knew us as people as well as teachers. It seemed strange that their first introduction to us came from a letter from the local authority, not from us. It was carefully worded, quite pleasant but rather legalistic in tone. Parents usually brought it along with them on their initial interview with me and it did, sometimes, cause consternation which I had to assuage. Here is the letter:

INNER LONDON EDUCATION AUTHORITY
Dear *Mr and Mrs Smith,*
EDUCATION ACTS 1944 TO 1971
SPECIAL EDUCATIONAL TREATMENT
Under the Education Act, 1944, the Authority has a duty to provide schools with special facilities for children who for any reason cannot properly benefit from attending ordinary schools. The same Act also makes parents responsible for ensuring that their children receive efficient full-time education suitable to their age, aptitude and ability.
As the result of a recent medical examination of your child
. . . *Claudette* . . . It is considered that he/she cannot make satisfactory progress in an ordinary school, but should attend a special school where the classes are small and the teachers are particularly experienced in giving the help your child needs.
. . . *Downsview School* . . . *Downs Road, E5* . . . would seem to be a suitable school and I should like you to take . . .

Claudette . . . to see the Headmaster/Headmistress . . . *Mr Wakefield* . . . at the school at . . . *10* . . . am/pm on . . . *Thursday 10 May 1973* . . . with a view to his/her admission. Please take this letter and your child's birth certificate with you.

If you do not agree with this suggestion or if you would like to know anything more about it, or if you intend to make suitable private arrangements for your child's special educational treatment, I hope that you will come and talk the matter over with me or one of my staff.

The progress of all children in special schools is kept under careful review to make sure that they are in the right type of school. Those who have made sufficient progress can return to ordinary school.

If I do not hear from you I shall assume that you will keep the appointment at the school as suggested above.

Yours sincerely,

A very cursory glance at this letter makes plain the cause of parental concern: 'As the result of a recent medical examination of your child . . . it is considered that he or she . . .' For many parents a medical examination seemed to imply that the decision was made because of some physical debility or even worse, some genetic deficiency. There is little to indicate here that the referral process included reports from teachers, head teachers and sometimes psychologists. In many instances the parents themselves were the prime instigators of the proceedings; this was particularly the case with withdrawn, retarded children.

'I've tried for two years to get my Janice here. OK, I knew she was quiet in school; quiet, but slow they said she was. Yes, too quiet, they didn't see her at home, keeping us up half the night frettin' and worryin' and all the crying before she left for school each day. I had to take her there myself every day and I knew she was getting nowhere.'

There were some enormously difficult issues to overcome at this initial interview, there were some questions (not always asked) that were impossible to answer. Sometimes parents asked for an immediate prognosis as to their child's development even before they had been in school. Each case was different. I supposed the aim for some children was a long-term curative one, and for others it was a question of two or three years' social, emotional and educational rehabilitation before returning them better-equipped to cope with secondary comprehensive education. All parents were well-informed of their right of appeal against special school placement. In four years, only one parent did appeal. Most of them were anxious for the placement, and indeed, many of them had pressured the authority for it. I did find out that the parent who appealed against placement won the appeal. I also know that the child concerned, whilst in ordinary school, was most unhappy. His brothers and sisters had all achieved a measure of scholastic success which he (through no fault of his own) had been denied. It seems sadistic that a child of eight years can write himself off as a failure on such tepid terms of reference. It was often necessary to wean parents away from the idea that their children were failures. Occasionally, they reinforced the failure themselves, even during their first visit to the school. The most concerned mothers have sat in my room, drinking their tea and calmly and sweetly declaring, 'Oh, my Jean she's six and can read better than him, and Francis she's eight, well she can do all sorts of things, her sums are good and anything in the house she can manage, and laugh, the things she comes out with. But my John, he's the eldest, don't seem interested in anything very much. As he's the only boy 'is Dad's ever so disappointed.'

I looked at John, who was winding up the toy robot on the cupboard. The passive face showed no trace of injury or humiliation; perhaps he was now immune to this kind of gentle but destructive denigration, perhaps not.

'Give him time and he might not disappoint you later on. I'd like to see you in three months and I will let you know how we feel about him. Of course you can call in any time . . .'

It was essential that parents felt secure with us, visiting us or staying the day with us. Once they felt secure, co-operation was much more forthcoming. At times this verged on dependence, particularly when parents themselves were under emotional or financial stress. There were two or three families who had more than one child attending the school. One such family always suffuses me with a warm glow of pleasure whenever I think of them.

It wasn't really necessary for Mrs Coogan to attend for an admission interview for Norman. Her daughters, Janet (ten) and Mary (eight), already attended the school and I had known Norman since he was three as she had always brought him along with her on her many visits to the school. At five she had wanted his name 'put down on our list' but I suggested that he should attempt ordinary school first and pointed out that I could not admit him just like that. I knew that she liked visiting the school and enjoyed the sense of occasion. Promptly at 10.00 am she arrived, beaming with pride, her six and a half year old son clinging to one arm and a carrier bag on the other. Norman appeared more of a weight than the bag and she entered my room looking like scales that were out of balance, the balance being in favour of the child. Whatever her difficulties (and they were many), the scales were always tipped in this fashion.

'Oh, I've had such a game gettin' here this mornin', I've got my flat – two bedrooms there is, one for me and the girls and one for Norman. Ain't there Norman? You seen it this mornin' didn't yer? Tell Mr Wakefield about the flat Mrs Block got for us. We ain't got no stairs neither, 'ave we?'

Norman interrupted at this point. It was difficult to understand his description as he spoke quickly and the speed of his delivery plus the severity of his speech defect difficulty forced me to concentrate all my attention on him. His mother must have picked up a studied frown from me.

'Ah, hardly anybody can understand him, but I can, so can

Mary and Janet. Then we're his family, we would, wouldn't we?' she added triumphantly. 'I'm ever so pleased he passed the examination to come here, Mrs Block says he can see a speech lady twice a week to help him with his talking, he can see her here at school can't he?'

I nodded and smiled assurance.

'Yes, the flat's lovely, we move in on Thursday, she's been good to me that Mrs Block. We've always been in one room before, I'm not having him back.'

I knew the pronoun referred to her husband. I didn't say anything. He had left her on three previous occasions, each time returning for board, comfort and lodging and giving nothing in return. There was an expression of finality in her face and I felt that her marital limpet had finally been cast adrift. She consolidated my thoughts.

'I don't love him no more, I've got the children, me own place, and I know he's had anuvver woman. It's not the same after that.'

She wasn't asking any questions, so I didn't offer any answers. I was pleased because I didn't know the answers anyway. Her children made her extremely happy, she loved to be in their company and motherhood for her was warm, fulfilling and total. In this sense her marriage had not been a complete disaster or failure, she was a successful mother who had achieved her success against very difficult odds. She began to rummage through her bag and took out a buff-coloured form.

'This letter is a different one from the one they sent me when Janet and Mary came here, look.'

She handed me the letter. A glance told me that it was, in fact, from the housing department. I knew that Mrs Coogan couldn't read; she had never discussed this with me, but always managed to present her 'forms' for me to peruse in this subtle manner.

'It's from the Housing Department; you have to state your

husband's income, his wages, how much he gets and brings home.'

She laughed.

'He never brought anything home. If he did, I never saw it. I can tell them the colour of his eyes and that's it. Can you write in the bits for me? You do it ever so quick, it'll take me all night to do the first page. I'll tell you somethin' Mr Wakefield, I can't read nor write meself. What with one thing and another, I've never had the time and I had hard times myself when I was little. I usually get a friend to do all this sort of thing for me, but it means everybody knows your business and she's not that much better than me at it, and that's not saying much.'

She smiled as she spoke, but the modulation of her voice and the expression on her face registered apology as well as need. I began to fill in the form for her, while presenting my plan as casually as I could.

'We have all your children here now, Norman can start today. You can come in and see them when you like. They're lovely children, I expect you're very proud of them. I know they think the world of you.'

She came over and took the form from my desk.

'Thank you, yes I'll miss them. I've always had one at home with me, it's company like and we're all good friends, you know. We do everything together of an evening.'

'You could come in of an afternoon and help Mr Foster, he's very good at teaching reading you know, he has a game in his room which teaches you to read and write. If you help your Janet, it wouldn't take you long to learn yourself and nobody would know about it. Mr Foster would love to have you helping in his class, it would be no trouble. Other mothers come in. Mrs Wilson will be here, and Mrs Graham.

'Is Mrs Wilson the pretty blonde lady that sees the children on to the coach?'

I nodded.

'Yes, I like her, it wouldn't be too much bother for you would it? I've never really had a chance before because classes for older people are in the evening and I couldn't leave the kids. Anyhow, I'm shy of going to classes, but I would come here.'

'That's settled it then, come on Wednesday, Thursday and Friday afternoons. You will be doing us a favour – it's no problem at all.'

Norman by this time had made his own way to the reception class. The building was not strange to him and he had entered school without apprehension or trauma.

Mrs Coogan had risen to leave. She offered to post some letters for me and to pop some muddied football shorts in the launderette. I accepted the offer as part of our domestic arrangements. These 'domestic' terms had broken the bonds of adult illiteracy and all the fears and misunderstandings that went with it. As Mrs Coogan left, Norman was already without shoes and socks dancing in the hall. He walked over to where she stood in the doorway. A huge dog bounded forward and began barking angrily at a group of children who were sketching the growing skyscraper flats and cranes outside the buildings. Three of the girls dropped their drawing boards and cowered in fright against the wall as the dog growled and sniffed his way around them. Mrs Coogan picked up a stick and walked towards the animal.

'G-e-r-r-off, g-e-r-r-off,' she shouted. She threw the stick on to the demolition site and the dog was happy to chase after it. I watched her collect the drawing boards, comfort and reassure the girls and admire their drawings before she left for the Post Office. Yes, she would be fine. I suppose when she can read fluently, the first book will be something for her children to listen to rather than something for herself, yet so close is this family that joy and sorrow are always collective and if her children are happy, then so is Mrs Coogan. She isn't learning to read to please the housing manager, her errant husband, the electricity board, herself or me. The main reasons for her projected efforts are Norman, Janet and Mary and they are as good a reason as any. Other parents too, have made enormous personal sacrifices in order to help their children.

A close scrutiny of David Willington's notes filled me with dismay. A pronounced physical deformity seemed to be coupled with a severe mental and emotional retardation. A great deal of medical care and examination had gone into finding the cause of his developmental difficulties but in spite of all the examinations and testing, there was nothing to prove that any actual brain damage existed or, indeed, that his retardation was in any sense genetic. He had been given a generous 'trial' period in a sympathetic infants school, but his achievement and progress there had only confirmed the previous psychological and medical diagnosis: 'A child of extremely low potential who will almost certainly fall within the ESN (severe) category. However, a trial in an ESN school should be proffered and if the transfer to Day (severe) is pending, then it needs to be approached with great care as parents may be resistant to the idea.' I had gone through the notes with Betty Krever, the teacher in charge of the reception class. She would often find details that I overlooked, she would be cautionary when I was overenthusiastic, yet hopeful when I found a situation bleak. There was no fuss or bother to Betty, yet her eye for detail remained clear and uncluttered. She had worked with Dr Keynell at the Wolfson Centre before coming to Hackney; she was a most skilled teacher, as well as being more knowledgeable than anyone else I had ever met with regard to the education of very young retarded children.

'This looks pretty grim doesn't it?'

I don't know whether I was asking for her sympathy or offering it. After all, she would be more totally concerned with the child than me and any success or failure in school would rest largely on her efforts. By the set of her mouth I knew that she had found something hopeful and come to an inward decision. Her face is rather plain except where she is expounding ideas or telling stories to children. Then the dark brown eyes flash, the mouth changes the simplest words to something of interest and fascination and her whole face becomes animated and changeable. At these times she is beautiful.

'Let's wait till he is here, the parents seem very interested.' She pointed to comments the parents had made, which were contradictory to the medical reports. 'Perhaps we could work with the parents more intensely, the language development ought to be better than it is and . . .' She had put the gloomy medical prognosis out of her mind, and found a chink of light and was going to pursue it. I left her room as she began a story. Her maxi-length skirt had got caught up on a desk as she gesticulated, there was a smudge of blue paint on the side of her face and she had become beautiful.

The next day the Willingtons arrived promptly at 11.00 am. I had completed the assembly and they were waiting in my room when I returned. It was unusual for both parents to attend. This meant that father had taken time off from work; it also showed practical evidence of interest in his son's well-being and future. They were a handsome couple: he swarthy-complexioned, bold-featured and care-worn, but proud, with thick dark hair kept well in place by more than enough Brylcreem. She came across more warmly. She smiled as she greeted me and pushed the blonde curls and ringlets away from a face which proved that some women can look much more than attractive at forty plus. The smile was unforced, warm and friendly. Our interview was interrupted before any verbal overtures could be made; our social courtship had been confined to smiles which had come mainly from Mrs Willington. Sobbing and cries of anguish outside forced me to excuse myself for a moment. Two infants had quarrelled at the onset of play-time. I listened to the arguments of both children and finally all three of us decided that blame was equally proportioned. The problem was simply solved as they both agreed to help the cooks in laying the knives and forks. Grievance and planned vendetta were lost in diversion and domesticity.

'I'm sorry I've kept you waiting, but it's as well to sort out these things early.' I could hear the children playing outside the office window as I sat down, took out Andrew's notes and placed them on the desk before me.

'That's all right, we understand.' Mr Willington spoke abruptly, but without impatience and I felt that he did understand. He moved forward on his chair and waited for me to begin. In spite of the preparation that I had given to the interview, I was still somewhat nervous and Mr Willington's intensity did not help me in this respect. I began to talk and could almost hear words in my own defence hidden behind the professional jargon which we sometimes call objectivity.

'Well, I have gone through David's notes very carefully and it would seem that he is very backward indeed, that is, it appears that he will be well behind all the children here. From what I can gather, he will probably find it difficult to manage at this school. Of course this might make him most unhappy and in this respect we might not be able to help
· him. There is another school for children who cannot manage here and perhaps his particular needs could be better met there. In any event, I am prepared to give him a trial period here and we will let you know at very regular interviews, how he is progressing . . .'

I talked on and on in this vein and was finally cut short by Mr Willington shaking his head and saying 'No'. I was relieved and quite pleased to be silenced. I listened.

'Look, I know what you're talking about, those schools you're referring to, they was called training centres. They've become schools since April. I know all about it and I've no complaints against them, I'm sure the people there do a good job, but I'm telling you my David can do better than that. I know you won't believe me, you'll think I'm saying it because he's my son, well, in some respects maybe I am, what father wouldn't? But apart from that I *know* he can do better than you and they (he pointed to the reports on my desk) think he can. OK, you're goin' to say, and go on about your experience and talk about them tests – but have you ever had a child at home with you all the time? Have you watched him and recorded what he's done and what he's not done for seven years, well have you? And another thing . . .'

Mrs Willington put her hand on Mr Willington's arm, restraining him gently as his voice grew louder. I felt better now, as Mrs Willington spoke.

'Kenny, let Mr Wakefield have a say . . .'

'No Kenny, you go on a bit more, I'll listen.' We all laughed and Kenny went on some more.

'No, seriously, Mr Wakefield, he can do much more than they give him credit for, for instance, he can take messages. I can send him to the shops on his own – and we are on a busy main street and that's not easy for a kiddy of his age. And when I'm working on my cab, he'll help and he's no trouble and if I explain what I'm doing, he understands. Nobody's going to tell me that my son's a cabbage, because he's not, I know he's not.'

Babs Willington took up the running, more gently persuasive than Kenny.

'He can be helpful in the house and my other children are very good with him. David is the youngest, then I have two daughters, Sharon, who will be leaving school soon, and my Carol, she's twelve and she helps David a lot. What Kenny says is true, David surprises me with what he comes out with sometimes.'

Kenny excused himself and left the room to collect David, who was waiting outside with one of his older sisters. Babs seized the opportunity to offer more placation.

'Kenny doesn't mean to get angry, when you know him he's just the opposite, it's only when he cares a lot about something and he tends to get a bit het up about it then; but his work gives him a lot of aggravation, cab-driving is a very worrying business. You'll understand, because I suppose your job's not without it.'

Kenny came in with his small blonde-haired son and introduced us immediately. I tried to establish a rapport with the boy, but none of the usual openings worked. He didn't want to play with any of the toys offered and all attempts at any kind of conversation were left suspended in the air. His reactions were not dull or bovine, they were just non-existent. He was rarely still in the room but always became static at father's command. The quick conclusion to this might be that the boy was in fear of his father, yet I was reasonably sure that this was not the case. When Kenny talked, David listened, and sometimes added small contributions to the conversation; his attention (which with others was negligible) was centred and contained. With these thoughts in mind I had no reason to disbelieve the Willingtons and as I escorted all the family to the classroom, I experienced my first shaft of optimism as to the child's future. Once again, the instant telepathy machine between father and son that I had witnessed before came into force. Usually, parents would spend some time, perhaps half a day, or a complete day, with their children, both sides feeling insecure about the parting. This was not the case with David Willington. His father took both his hands, looked him in the eyes and said,

'I've got to go to work now, David.'

'And Babs as well?' asked David.

'Yes, and Babs. You stay here and we'll see you later – we'll meet you off the bus. It's a big bus.'

David accepted this without argument or tears. There was no sign of distress as he waved goodbye to his parents and disappeared into the Wendy House.

'I'm sorry I have to say a rushed cheerio. I'm due at a meeting and I'm already late.' As I spoke, I was assembling papers and pushing files into my brief-case. 'You know that you can contact me whenever you like about David and if we are worried about anything, we will contact you. I would like you to attend all the parents' meetings and activities if it's possible . . .'

'Where do you have to get to now?' Kenny spoke in his usual practical manner. I told him that it was at another school in the south of Hackney.

'Don't panic then, I'll give you a lift in the cab, it's parked outside. You're not a driver are you?'

It was more of a statement than a question, and I immediately acquiesced to both his offer and his insight. The ride in the cab dispelled any anxiety that I might have been feeling about being late and I half listened to Kenny who talked about his own job and the particular worries it gave him. The other half of me was thinking about his son. Kenny's approach towards David seemed to work – his requests and demands were abrupt, his manner was friendly but firm, and the language he used was economical, always related and to the point. He had not patronised his son and whenever possible, he had given him the opportunity to accept simple responsibilities. I climbed out of the cab at Bethnal Green Tube Station, and thanked them for the morning. They reciprocated my sentiments, and I made my way to the meeting with the feeling that I had learned more about the possibilities of educating David Willington from his father than I had from his medical notes.

Within a matter of days, Betty Krever was reinforcing this matter-of-fact approach in the classroom. David's attention span in this early period appeared to be void. He would wander aimlessly around the classroom, only occasionally centring his interest and even then he did not sustain it long enough for it to be constructive. Betty Krever is never easily deterred. The more difficult the situation, the better she seems to like it. I have heard her husband refer to her as a 'fudge-pot'. Translated by him, this means that she has to put together all the details before she considers the total score. If the details don't fit, then she will fiddle about until they do. She led David into a structured learning situation, often breaking his seemingly aimless wandering by taking his hand and marshalling him into an activity. This might mean sitting with him and sharing what he was doing as well as supplying a flow and interchange of words to fit the activity. It was delightful to watch, and it was equally pleasing to watch Kathy Graham, our nursery assistant, emulate her approach, when Betty herself was working with other children.

An assembly in an all-age school is a happy way of beginning the day. The huge age range does not diminish the interest, but increases it. Older children are fascinated by the performances and achievements of younger ones and an adolescent singing, with guitar accompaniment, does not produce the soporific stare in five-year-olds that many TV programmes engender. David, however, was not captivated by our performances. On the contrary, he gave us one of his own by careering round, a quarter of the way through the proceedings, making bleeping noises and high-pitched buzzing sounds. On the first few occasions he disappeared from view after he had created mild chaos, with Betty chasing after him in hot pursuit. She never entered his game of hide-and-seek, she simply found him, took his hand and led him back with the kind of off-hand practical application that goes into making a cup of tea. Then she sat with him at the side of the hall.

'Betty, do you think there's much point in David coming . . .' She never let me finish the negative question.

'Give him time,' she would say, implying that I was wasting hers mentioning that she might give up. For several weeks she sat with him at the side of the hall, occasionally whispering information to him, presumably sharing what was going on in the hall with him. They were confidants within the collective situation, rather like two football fans exchanging ideas or apprehensions over the ensuing match. I wondered how Betty would score her winning goal and get David to sit with the rest of the class. I knew that her timing was perfect, and if the chance arose, she would not miss it.

'Class I have been working on something special for us all this week and they are going to play and sing it for us this morning.' Jeremy Baker hitched his guitar on his shoulder as she spoke and nodded to the fifteen multi-coloured infants. Their instruments were laid out on the hall stage: there were clarinas, tambourines, drums and home-made maraccas and shakers. Each child selected his or her instrument, and the orchestra and chorus were assembled in less time than it takes the Philharmonic to sneeze. We were treated to a rousing version of 'Go Down Moses'. It wasn't until the second chorus of the encore that I noticed that David was part of the orchestra, complete with maraccas. The orchestra received its applause and Betty praised David quietly and directed him to sit with the rest of the class, which he did. She left the hall and I continued. David remained seated until it was time to leave with the others and he has accepted this arrangement ever since.

Mrs Willington had offered to act as relief attendant on our coach rounds if ever any attendant was sick or ill. Eventually, the situation became a permanent one and later she joined us as a full-time paid attendant help, working in the classroom or playground wherever she might be needed. Her presence within the school probably added to David's feelings of security and his improvement continued. Betty would relate anecdotes which she took as proof of his intellectual development.

'He gave me the funniest piece of news this morning, they have been making a film in his street, advertising some breakfast cereal, apparently David is in it and he's been having a whale of a time over the weekend, they built a decorated cart and . . .' or she might say, 'Just look at this drawing, he's got the crane in the right position and there's the chain see, and look, there's the man in charge.'

I accepted her word, but for my own part, I had seen no improvement except for David's observance of certain social rituals within the school, coupled with an ability to relate to other children and adults more quickly than he had done before.

A trip to Canvey Island enlightened me. Situated in the mouth of the Thames estuary, nearer Essex than Kent, this strange place was once a mecca of resorts for London's East End. Bungalows and disjointed estates seem to sprout every-where, small avenues come to abrupt endings and the bingo halls on the tiny sea-front are near-derelict by the end of September. Somehow it exerts a fascination on a first visit, perhaps it is the jellied eels, it might be the semi-resident East End caravanners who re-visit loyally each year and inject some feeling into the place. A huge chemical works looms on the horizon and stickers on cars and in shop windows exhort, 'Keep Canvey clear of oil refineries'. The place is almost reminiscent of an old music hall making a last wobbly effort to survive. It was one of the thousand caravans that attracted me there. It belonged to the Willingtons. Babs had said that I could use it if ever I wanted some peace and quiet and I took her at her word one weekend in late September. Kenny insisted on driving me down there in his cab one Friday evening after school. They saw me settled in and secure, and said they would arrive to collect me on the Sunday. The weather, like their charity, was warm and undemanding and I enjoyed the solitude. The Willingtons (as dependable as ever) arrived at lunch-time, bringing Carol and David with them. After lunch, we spent the day together walking on the beach and visiting the rather jaded amusement park. It was during these few hours that I saw what Betty and Kenny saw – an independent David, a David who could take decisions, go on errands, a David who had a sense of direction, and a David who was beginning to converse. I attached myself to the family for these few hours before leaving and felt better for it. As we were driving home in the darkness, sitting in the front of the cab, I broke into the conversation.

'David is doing much better than I ever thought he would, Kenny.'

It was more of a confession than anything else. Kenny delivered the absolution swiftly.

'Yes, he is, I know he is,' and he turned and smiled as he spoke and I was pleased to feel humble; with parents like this, could any child fail?

Flora Maynard's parents reversed this question. She was one of the most attractive little girls that I have ever seen. At the first interview with her mother, she stood perfectly still, her head held slightly on one side, a gentle, perplexed frown veiling the nine-year-old face and all her clothes, including her shoes, too big for her very thin frame. Mrs Maynard complained throughout the interview and showed not the slightest trace of affection for her daughter. In school, Flora managed to overcome some of her depression and we would witness a lovely slow smile that would surely ignite the coldest emotions. Perhaps her mother and her stepfather never saw it. Each month Mrs Maynard would come to school and ask if we could 'put Flora away'. I tried everything conceivable to get Mrs Maynard to like her daughter, but she remained unmoved and cold. I never managed to see Mr Maynard. None of the children liked the long summer holiday much, but Flora was the only child who wept at its onset. Hazel (our Educational Welfare Officer) visited the home often and after Flora had been with us for just over a year, Hazel spoke to me about her last visit.

'They say she causes trouble and that she is splitting the family, but the plain truth of the matter, Tom, is that they just don't want her and Flora knows it. Mrs Maynard is coming to see you tomorrow, she says she can't cope with her at home any longer.'

Hazel flushed as she spoke, probably because, like me, she felt impotent with regard to the situation.

I spoke quietly, 'Flora has asked me and Mary (her teacher) if she can go away to school. I think I might grant her request.'

Hazel nodded: 'I think you will have to, Tom, there won't be any alternative.'

'She is always standin' round, always complainin' when I ask her to do anything. My husband don't like her around with that long face.' Mrs Maynard continued her usual denigration and this time I didn't try to counter it with information about Flora's good behaviour in school, her charm, her smile. It was hopeless trying to be positive in the face of such total negation. It would be impossible for me to prove that these parents had neglected this child, in spite of her thinness and depression.

'If you can put her away, I will be happy, she is a great worry and trouble to us.'

I spoke tersely. 'There are boarding schools, there is one small one that I know of that I think Flora will like, but she will not be 'put away'. It would be nice for her if you could visit her weekends; in time, you might get to be fond of her like we are here.'

Mrs Maynard poked about in her bag and pushed a boiled sweet into her mouth.

'Yes, send her there. I don't like her.' She shook her head as she spoke her last sentence before she left. 'I don't want her.'

My secretary, who had clothed Flora whilst she was at school with us, had overheard the conversation. She wasn't crying but was near to it.

'Will she go, Tom?'

I nodded. 'Social grounds' was what I heard myself saying.

Mrs Maynard would not have been interested in a formal, written end-of-term report. Such a report would be of little use to Mrs Coogan and not of much consequence or meaning to Mrs Willington. Class positions would have been impossible to determine. We saw most parents and progress was discussed, books shown, problems sorted out at a less artificial level of communication than the written word. However, we all felt the need for a letter each term. This came from the class teacher with a comment from me, plus a section left for parents to say what they thought in reply. This report was sent to a mother who was never stinting in her criticism of her little boy and found little of value in anything he did:

DOWNSVIEW SCHOOL

Headmaster: Tom Wakefield   *Class Teacher*: Lis Munson

GENERAL PROGRESS REPORT

Name: John J.

Dear Mr and Mrs J.,

I am sure you will be pleased to hear that John is working very hard at school and that his work is getting better every day. He is trying very hard with his reading, writing very neat and quite long stories, and working very carefully in other subjects. He especially enjoys sewing and does it very well, as you will have seen from the piece which he brought home.

He is very kind to younger children and is trying hard to settle down. I am encouraging him to bring his work home to show you, as he so much wants you to be pleased with him, and I feel very strongly that he needs as much love and praise as you can give him at this stage so that the improvement may continue.

Headmaster

John has tried very hard this term. The more he is praised the more he does. A great deal of his good progress is due to Mrs Munson who is very fond of him.

Parental Comment (Please return this section if you wish)

....

This is not a critical letter. No sanctions are implied, yet it extends an open invitation to Mum to join in our pleasure and share our enthusiasm for her son's progress. Some reports were used to praise parents. One parent, in particular, was so self-effacing that we took every opportunity we had to support and encourage her. Her little girl had been most withdrawn on first attending school, but Mrs Bedford had conscientiously come along with her each day, until eventually Sheila was able to come unaccompanied and attended school willingly. Mrs Bedford always helped at functions and was the sort of mother who left before one could say 'thank you' – or, if you did thank her, 'Oh, it's nothing, nothing at all, I don't really think that I've done anything, but if you say it helps.' She openly complained of her own lack of confidence in herself and gave weekly practical demonstrations disproving her own theory. We all liked her very much.

Headmaster: Tom Wakefield   *Class Teacher*: Lis Munson
GENERAL PROGRESS REPORT
Name: Sheila Bedford
Dear Mr and Mrs Bedford,
    I am particularly pleased with Sheila, who has become very helpful and grown up. She is nearly always ready to do anything that other children do; even if it is an activity which she doesn't enjoy, she can usually be persuaded to join in.
    She is working very hard and her reading and writing are making good progress.
    I am sure that she will continue to improve with the encouragement she receives from you.
Headmaster
Thanks to your help and co-operation, Sheila has done very well this term. She should have no difficulty in entering the working world later on if she maintains her present rate of progress. I am sure that she will continue to improve with the combined support that she receives from home and school.

I once gave Mrs Bedford a box of chocolates after she had washed up piles of crockery that had marooned itself in the kitchen after a Christmas social. She found it difficult to accept the gift, but slowly we are convincing her that we think she is important and, what is more, she is beginning to realise this too. There is no postscript from me on this last letter. The parental comment is more explicit and its joyful economy covers more ground in forty words than I could realise in a chapter.

Headmaster: Tom Wakefield   *Class Teacher*: Lis Munson
GENERAL PROGRESS REPORT
Name: Rufus St Stephen

Dear Mrs St Stephen,

I am very pleased with Rufus, who has improved so much that he seems a different boy from the one I first met last September.

He is working very hard, reading well and writing long interesting stories without any help. He settles down quickly and does not need much supervision.

The greatest improvement is in his behaviour; he is becoming sensible, helpful and kind, does not fight so much as he used to and has quite a sense of humour. He also talks much more than he used to, especially about Lavinia! He is obviously very fond of her and loves to make presents for her.

I know you will be pleased about all this, particularly as you were so worried about him before Lavinia was born.

Headmaster

I know that this report will make you very happy, I have heard so much about the new baby, please bring her in to see us when you have the time.

Parental Comment (Please return this section if you wish)

I can't explain how pleased both my husband and myself felt when I read Rufus's report, I am really happy about him, oh, yes, I know he loves Lavinia, he wants her to grow very fast, so that they can both play together. From Lavinia was born, Rufus is a changed boy.   M. St Stephen

Very slowly, but most definitely over a period of three years, parents too became part of the community that the school represented. Earlier I referred rather acidly to romantic attitudes towards what was in the past referred to as 'working-class community feeling'. I had experienced it myself in the past and in many ways it was not so different from the present. The idea that woe, trouble, bad times and intense hardship bring marvellous endearments and unity against a poor and industrious background is a spurious one. Many people accept or accepted group situations by sacrificing and subjugating personal ideals and needs, not intrinsically for the betterment of the group or the community that they are in, but out of fear of it – fear of the sanctions it may place on them if they indulge in a free search for a more personal fulfilment. If a community engenders this kind of 'spiritual' poverty, that squashes and squeezes the life blood from an individual, then the patiently awaited cultural breakthrough will never come. Writers will continue to produce disillusioned and angry plays and novels flecked with despair that might occasionally verge on the compassionate and some weary professors may even try to improve their bank balances by proving that 'certain' groups are born dull. Born bludgeoned might be nearer the truth.

In this sense, we did not become a part of a community, we became a satellite community that contributed to the main source whilst maintaining its own rights as to influences and values. In the wider context, I suppose our contribution was tiny and during the holidays I sometimes wondered if it made much difference whether or not we existed at all. I wonder how it has come about that holidays are so separate from school or, in broader terms, that holidays are so unrelated to the educational process. There is something sad about the idea of children cheering at the end of term. Does this constitute a release for them, like chickens let out to run in the yard? If it does, then I feel that there is something wrong with 'school' as we know it.

The idea of comprehensive education is still as attractive and proper as ever, but if we are going comprehensive, then let us really go. At present, we are still viewing education in chronological stages and even these are further mummified into categories such as nursery, infant, primary, secondary, further and adult. Educational establishments still reflect these inflexible groupings, so that a nursery school is a nursery school and no more, and an adult education institute remains a place for adults. In the present situation, I feel that we are becoming more and more the products of our own environment, rather than the creators of it. Unless we stop the rot, we shall see more derelict people as well as derelict buildings. Half-baked demonstrations by environmentalists, ecologists and sociologists will have little effect unless the pending urban nightmare passes to dream and then pleasant reality. The 'pleasant reality' would need a lot of feeding from birth and some sustenance could be provided by the setting up of the first all-age community schools in urban areas. Perhaps we could get rid of the word 'school' altogether, as far as education is concerned; the establishments that I foresee would probably not fit the label.

In a society where we are constantly warned about the dangers and even the sinfulness of waste, it seems to me that there is more wastage of human potential than any other growing commodity. An all-age school would need to be a storehouse of information, trades, skills, ideas, praise as well as critical response. Children from four to fourteen years, teachers as we know them now, parents and craftsmen, allied with trades, industry and welfare, would use such a centre simultaneously. There would need to be tremendous flexibility and experimentation with regard to the length and pattern of the centre's daily programme. There should be no need for the building ever to close before 9.30 pm at night and it ought to represent a permanent and fixed information centre for parents and children alike. I see no reason why a skill should not be bartered for an idea, or why trade know-how could not comfortably be exchanged for some differing philosophical outlooks. In this sense learning and the quest for further understanding and knowledge would assume a natural, utilitarian role to all people, which the present scheme of things denies the majority; and education might find a new realism.

8

A JOURNEY,
TWO PORTRAITS AND A BOTTLE OF GUINNESS

The children who came to us were of all ages, all shapes, all colours and all sizes. For different reasons they had come to us from infants or primary as well as comprehensive schools. Their problems and difficulties were never purely educational, yet we were accountable for their education and this we undertook as best we could. The teaching of reading presented us with many heartaches. It was impossible to adopt a single scheme as most of the children had already been following different schemes in their previous schools. Apart from these factors, many immigrant children found any learning situation difficult. We all discussed it endlessly, both formally and informally.

An atmosphere for creative learning was difficult to achieve with children who were so disintegrated. We decided that although a freedom of choice of subjects should be available for the children, it was necessary for us to structure that choice to the needs of individual children as well as groups of children. If these children were to learn in a creative sense then they had to feel free to learn from a wide variety of sources and experiences. The younger children desperately needed to socialise and to share their experiences and findings, and they, too, needed to be allowed some choice in the pursuit of an activity.

Before the school had opened, I remember squelching

through mounds of mud surveying the play and recreation areas with the site manager. He pointed to two round open spaces in the middle of the rather narrow infants' playground.

'This is designated for herbaceous plants and those delightful little border rockery-type ones; and the other is for roses.'

'Roses?' I asked.

'Yes, we will choose some of the hardier varieties.'

'I don't want roses, I want climbing logs there. Tell your department it's cheaper my way, that will settle it. On the other side I'm having a sandpit and a slide and another climbing frame. The staff all agree with me.'

'But the order has gone through now, you can't do this.'

'Yes I can, these children must learn to play before they can look at a rose. They will be looking at roses eventually.'

We did have our own garden, rabbits and hamsters, later. The planning and the choice of flowers were left to us.

Our reading programmes were put together in much the same way : reading shelves were compiled which linked reading books with all the schemes that the children had encountered before and most children, after finding a security that they had not known before, chose a reading series which suited them. This paid hefty dividends and the rate of increase in reading ability surprised and pleased all of us. There were no 'special' methods, just a great deal of extra care.

We felt that it was imperative for us to meet other teachers in the area, for two reasons. If we were transferring children back to ordinary schools, then it would be as well to know which ones were sympathetic to their needs. And if schools were sending children to us, they might have some idea of what we would try to do for the children whom they felt they could not help.

Children, parents and teachers teach teachers to teach. Unfortunately, all three groups operate for much of their time in isolation from one another. It would have been impossible for us to visit all the schools that our catchment area covered.

We could not get to the teachers in those schools, therefore we had to get them to come to us. April 1970 helped us enormously, when the local education authority decided that all schools should celebrate 100 years of education (passing of State Education Act 1870–1970). We asked if our school could be chosen that particular year as the school to welcome new teachers into the area. The occasion instigated a major school project, the theme of which was quite simple – it was 100. The walls were covered with pictorial history charts, number apparatus, a gigantic centipede with its full quota of legs crawled across the hall ceiling. At the time appointed, the building was flooded with teachers who showered accolades on the children over their cups of tea. There was a distinct feeling of pride when Peter pointed to the fourteenth leg of the centipede, turned his sparkling black complexion towards the lady teacher holding his hand, and said –

'I done that, no not that one, the orange with the black on the feet.'

Evening lectures and seminars were arranged for teachers through the local authority's teaching centre. They were held at the school. We were not too hopeful about attendance: how could we expect teachers to tramp over to us after an exhausting day's work? Our first lecture was entitled 'Aggression in City Children'. I thought it would probably put most teachers off, as they would probably already have experienced half a week of that particular commodity. I was proved quite wrong. At 4.30 pm, teachers began arriving. We catered for them and gave them a cup of tea, so that before they listened they had time to relax and chat. By 5.00 pm the building was full. How dated the Giles cartoon figures seem, when one looks at teachers today. There was a complete age range, in fact within the building there were thousands of years of teaching experience. There were beautiful girls with long hair and flowing dresses who could have stepped out of a pre-Raphaelite painting; young men with black hair and beards to match, and a striking absence of the 'tweed' image which is still being foisted upon us.

Younger teachers were sandwiched between older ones and the building buzzed; the lectures proved successful and since then we have always held at least five each term. The more I watch and listen to teachers sharing experience and concern, the more I am convinced that a comprehensive school must be all-age to be truly comprehensive. Ideally the roll should be about 600 and the age range be from four to fourteen years. If this could ever become a reality, teaching methods would improve, behaviour disorders would appear less evident and growth in all areas would not be restricted to terms of chronological/educational measurement. Technical colleges, sixth form colleges, polytechnics could maintain relationships with such schools, and career and leisure activities could easily be 'pipelined' to them in later adolescence.

Many of the teachers attending were surprised to hear a few harsh facts, one being that 10 per cent of the whole present school population could, if necessary, be classified as educationally sub-normal; of that 10 per cent, only 1 per cent is given special school provision. In urban areas, this 1 per cent would probably have an extra handicap added to the social ones that they already carried. Disturbed behaviour and speech defects and mild epilepsy were the commonest of these, and over a third of our school intake carried this extra burden. Epilepsy presented subtle difficulties as far as working prospects were concerned. May Hadley, one of the attendant helpers, had an epileptic son of nineteen and she stated the case more succinctly than I could. She usually talked at play and recreation times, whilst we were on duty together.

'My Eddie has got another interview this week, he didn't get anywhere with the last one. You don't want to hear all this from me, do you? You've got enough on your plate 'ere.'

'Yes I do, May.'

'Well at the last place, they said they would let him know.

They always say that. We haven't heard anything and I know the letter when it comes. We've had them before.' She mimicked the letter: 'Sorry to inform you that the vacancy has already been filled. If any occur at a later date, we will inform you.' She spoke, not with bitterness, but with candour. 'And I've heard that before, he's got another interview this week. I've told 'im to say nothing about the fits. I don't know whether I'm right or not, but he's not had a turn for four years now. Honestly, you don't know what to say about it, if you tell the truth he gets nowhere and if I tell a lie, he might suffer for it later. I have one boy and he has to have this, it don't seem fair at times. He was no trouble at school apart from the fits.' She laughed. 'I wish he had of been, he might have come here then; but you weren't 'ere then was you. Oh, Ernie (her husband) and me have had some terrible times when the fits came on, but the tablets seem to have stopped them all now, touch wood; but I wish Eddie would go out more. He had a girl friend, but it's all over, to tell you the truth I'm glad 'cos I thought she was common. Anyhow, I'll let you know how he gets on.'

Eddie got the job and held it for one month. During that time he was never absent or late and agreed to work overtime whenever the firm required it of him. His dismissal gives cause for conjecture. It may be that he proved inadequate, that his phenobarbitone dosage left him too slow. I don't know. May, his mother, was again left with the problem and I believe the humour and tenderness of this particular lady will finally overcome it, strenuous high jump that it is. It is impossible to talk about children without looking at some of the adults around them. May Hadley was one such adult, another was Margaret Estelle Gates, Deputy Head, known to all as Maggie.

Margaret Gates's own family were all grown up, the eldest son being in his thirties. On all forms requesting her age, I truthfully wrote 'adult'. No hot-air machine had ever touched her iron-grey hair, which was simply washed and cut. She did boast once to us all that a famous West End hairdresser had cut and shaped it, but someone callously remarked that it looked the same as it always did, so from then on she presumably continued to cut it herself. Apart from being deputy head and a class teacher, she was also responsible for girls' games and swimming and always undertook to go on school outings. If cartwheels were necessary to aid children's development, then she could have performed them. She was a specialist in needlework and art craft too, but had grown to enjoy class teaching more than any form of specialisation.

Any change suggested to her was at first greeted in a cautious manner.

'Oh, I couldn't do that my love, my maths are hopeless. I'll bet I'd make it interesting though; we could have our own shop in the corner over there. I want my own scales and the girls can do a weight watchers' thing. I'd like to send a group out just to compare prices and we can chart them when they get back. My boys could really go to town on this building, it's due for decoration this year. We could measure it, plan it, cost it, the lot.'

She continued charting out an excellent maths programme. When we were without a cookery teacher, she put on a checked apron and sallied forth with her own brands of culinary delights.

'You know, Tom, salads aren't easy. There's art in making salads and they can be cheap if you're careful.'

The most appetising salads were produced, artistic mosaics of vegetables and fruits. The children loved it all. However, during one period when she was probably being overenthusiastic, Maggie lopped off the end of her forefinger and came to my room shamefaced.

'Oh, look what I've done, none of the kids know, they are all OK, I'm so stupid. I was talking to Errol and my finger nearly joined the radishes before I knew what I was doing.'

The top of the finger was replaced by the hospital, but for

Maggie's own sake I removed her from the cookery-room from that day onward.

Formal staff meetings were held every Thursday morning before school started. Every day there were staff meetings during break-periods and at the end of the day we all gathered informally. May Hadley looked after us well on these occasions, bustling in with tea and bringing the warmth of a mother hen. Informal staff meetings proved the most productive. Policies were not hammered out, but woven, and direct confrontations were avoided; differences of opinion rarely caused any animosity and the staff enjoyed each other's company. Maggie was always supportive to younger and older teachers alike. Her wisdom and experience was unquestionable, but her most beguiling quality was probably her innocence.

One evening after a particularly punitive day, she startled us all.

'I'm going to Suffolk this weekend. There's the most lovely house there in the country.' She framed the house with her hands and flicked the trailing Indian scarf over her shoulder as she continued. 'There's a wild, natural-looking garden and at the bottom an orchard. It's just what I want for my old age.'

This was hardly the sort of comment we expected from a lady who swam in all weathers and even offered to run keep-fit classes for the staff. Betty Krever, the all-time realist, broke into Maggie's verbal raptures.

'Where are you going to get the money from? That sort of place will cost a fortune.'

This simple statement turned all attention towards Maggie, who lit a cigarette before replying. She puffed a cloud of smoke into the air.

'Well, I've got all that side of it tied up.'

'Have you been left some money then?' We all knew that Maggie's financial resources were permanently drained.

'I shall sell the house that I'm winning in this competition and use the money to buy the one in Suffolk. There's no need to look like that, this competition is a dead cert for me – and there, look, the first prize is a house.'

'What do you have to do to win?' Betty asked. 'It's not a crossword, is it?'

'No, it might have been made for me. All I have to do is write a slogan about this.'

Maggie produced a picture of a Guinness bottle. She often surprised us all in this way; not all of her schemes worked out exactly as planned. The previous year she had imbued us with a sense of urgency that every child should grow something. Her enthusiasm could not be checked, hundreds of bulbs arrived from kindly gardeners and firms and, in consequence, that spring the school building was flooded with potted crocuses and daffodils and we did not feel that we wanted even to look at a mustard and cress sandwich ever again. It was with a certain amount of disquiet and some misgivings that we viewed the picture of the Guinness bottle. There was to be no stopping her now.

'I don't expect you lot to understand, but I really enjoy my glass of Guinness after work. The taste, texture, it's balm to me.'

'What's your slogan?' asked Betty.

'I'm not saying; anybody could steal it, then I've lost my house haven't I?'

We waited, knowing full well that she was about to tell us.

'Well, I hope I can trust you all: "When I have my Guinness I know I am home." '

She waited for our response but, in answer, other teachers began to do domestic jobs about the staffroom: one washed cups and saucers, another began sorting out the notice board. Maggie was not daunted by our lack of optimism. Long after the results of the competition were declared, she still felt there might have been a mistake. A consolation prize would not have been acceptable to her, she does not have a country dream home, but at least she still has her glass of Guinness.

She always combined maturity with innocence so that whichever role she was playing on a certain day, basically she was always herself. I have seen her as the cookery expert in trim check print apron; as the games-field enthusiast, resplendent in royal blue track-suit; the cross-Channel swimmer; the expert fashion cutter with glasses suspended on a tape from round her neck. During the Christmas play period, we greeted a female Cecil B. de Mille or a Visconti. Her resources were endless, but in spite of this, her classroom was organised, lively, peaceful and exciting. Largely due to her care, there were no unwanted pregnancies in our building, no frightened child-mothers and little ignorance with regard to the beauty or harshness of the facts of life. She is a self-confessed atheist, yet looking at her, listening to her, watching her at work, I am sure that she will go on for ever and ever, thus defeating her own thesis.

Margaret Gates was probably even more effective as an educator out of school than in. She hated to miss an outing whether it was a concert at the Festival Hall or a trip to France for the day. Travelling with children was no odious task for her and she did not have to force or squeeze her sense of discovery or wonder for the benefit of the children, it was just there. The school took one group holiday each year for a week or a fortnight. This consisted of twenty-five children, two teachers and one mother who came along as an assistant. It meant that all the children could, at some stage during their time with us, have a holiday by the sea which was healthy and valuable in terms of experience and interest. The preparation was enormous. A family group of mixed age range was equipped and briefed by Maggie with military precision, yet the details were always presented carefully and gently. Parents came and discussed the forthcoming departures of their children and particular needs were sorted out before embarkation. We made a point of taking at least three or four eneuretic children along with us. Bet-wetting causes great misery and even guilt to children who are so afflicted, as well as to their parents. We eradicated the stigma involved before they left.

'Look, don't worry about it, we have special sheets to take along and Mrs Graham is going to sort everything out. If it does happen, nobody is going to be cross or angry with you. We just want you to enjoy this school journey, and we will enjoy it more if you come with us.'

These two weeks by the sea without stress or pressure did, in fact, cure many of them and in almost all cases, there was a cutting down in the frequency of occurrence. Departure from school was joyous and confident, with children happy to be going away and parents equally pleased to see them go. I usually visited the group for the weekend, accompanied by two or three other teachers. The hopfields of Kent had cleansed us of the city atmosphere before we reached the coast and arrived at the centre where our group was staying. Maggie had 'routed' us to the coast and then added –

'Just follow the Martello towers, after the fourth one along you will find us on the beach round about half-past one.'

The towers were a pretty useless investment as far as Napoleon was concerned, but they proved to be invaluable to us. After the fourth tower we were confronted with an endless expanse of pebble-sand beach which was broken up by a seemingly endless jigsaw of children. The Romney Marshes were deserted except for sheep, and it seemed that all human life had emptied itself on to the seashore.

'Perhaps it would be as well to wait for them at the centre until they get back. We'll never be able to find them amongst this lot.' I spoke testily, as I was disappointed at not being able to see them all on arrival.

'No, there they are, you can't miss them, look.' Sheelagh Pope pointed farther along the beach. 'They stand out, look there's Gilbert and I'm sure that's Errol sitting on the break-water.'

Our group was easily identified, the black, brown and ochre flesh was surrounded by pink and white forms and, for the first time, their colour in these surroundings set them visually apart. They were a focal point and, without any discussion or decisions, we three adults began to run towards them, jumping over sandcastles, puddles and half-empty bottles of suntan lotion. Errol spotted us from the breakwater and, like a true lighthouse, transmitted news of our coming without speaking a word. Within seconds they were all around us like tugboats.

'Mrs Gates ain't half tanned, wait till you see her, she's swimming with Joseph and Pauline and some of the others. Mr Goulden says the sea's too cold. I never knew Mrs Gates was a good swimmer.'

'We had a concert last night and there was a film on Tuesday night.'

'I didn't sleep the first night, Angela kept giggling and talking, I do now though, I'd never get up of a morning if I didn't, there's so much to do here, I can't believe we go back on Monday.'

'Oh, shut up about going back, Shirley. Here, Sir, you should have seen us on this Indian Railway this morning. It's not an Indian railway really, but it's not just a toy miniature thing either. The coaches and engine were ever so small and the journey to this lighthouse was miles away. It was so small this train, that if you leaned out of the carriages, you could nearly touch the sheep. They're everywhere round here. We saw one having a baby in the middle of the field. It sort of fell out of the big one's back and then it stood up.'

'We're in the sports tomorrow, some of the other schools are bigger than us.'

'Did you get my card? I sent one to Wilmer Bailey but she's not answered, she ain't half rotten.'

'Are you staying here tonight? Billy's got a girlfriend, she's from another school and there are French people here as well.'

This chequered diary of the week welcomed us to our party. They were preparing to leave the beach for lunch, there was no suntan lotion to remember, they were in no need of it, and towels and belongings were being carefully packed away. Maggie had emerged from the sea and had to be half-carried over the pebbles by the group of children that were swimming with her.

'Oh, I really envy people with good feet. I've never had beautiful feet you know, don't look at them, my toes make me sick. The water's cold but it's lovely when you get out.'

The accommodation was well situated; only the road separated it from the seashore. At one time it must have been an army barracks, although looking around I couldn't see how this bastion could ever have defended the exposed and rather bleak areas of the Romney Marsh coast from invaders. The present populace of children gave the place an atmosphere of settlement rather than occupation, but the heavily labelled dormitories somehow still gave it an air of regimentation and order which was out of keeping with both the coastline and its present inhabitants. A look at the inside of the dormitories dismissed these historical, pseudo-bucolic thoughts from my mind. Children, more than anything that lives, give immediacy to an environment or a situation. The wildest imagination could never have envisaged these rooms, in their present state, as army barracks. The wall space was not limited to pin-ups or pop stars, although some did look down on the scene in various states of musical agony or bliss. Five sections of the room were taken up with leisure or work tables, and these sections had done more for the dormitory than Robinson Crusoe did for his island. There were paintings of boats, lighthouses, sheep, flowers, sea and sky; collections of flowers, seaweed, shells and driftwood. Cartoon accounts of

trips and visits that they had made all reflected their awareness and sensitivity of their new environment. Maps were
always illustrated and brought to life with points like 'George
lost his haversack somewhere around here'. Maggie had organised them all into making diaries in school before the journey.
The choice of keeping a personal record or journal was
optional and its presentation was left to the children to decide.
They usually worked on them before meal-times and painting
and crayoning after supper seemed to be part of the cocoa,
pyjamas and slippers routine.

'Sir, Mrs Gates says stop messing about here and that she's
waitin' for you, she says we all have to eat together and you're
holdin' everybody up. We are goin' on the tram-line at three
o'clock, that's why you have to come now.'

'I think I've lost my keys, Winston, I put them near
the . . .'

'Mrs Gates told me to say to you that she's got them and
to hurry up . . .'

'Hold that for me then Winston, would you? Thanks, did
you say we were all going on a tram-line? Whatever are we
doing that for?'

'Mrs Gates says it's great, you bounce on it and tipple over
in the air, she's been on it before, there's a man coming to
show us how to do it all, Joe Duberry says he knows anyhow
'cos he's seen one on television.'

At three in the afternoon I was comforted to see a trampoline and relieved that Maggie's rampant imagination had not
extended to us all taking over a tram-line in some form or
another. We all sat around the contraption that was due to
add the new dimension of flight to our movements and all of
us bubbled with anticipation and excitement. Our instructor,
who lived forty minutes' journey away, arrived exactly on
time. He was zipped into blue tracksuit from ankle to throat,
above which was a face of granite, topped with crew-cut hair
that was more severe than the frowning face. He spoke to the

air in a loud booming voice, addressing none of us, and proceeded to destroy all the interest that we had built up.

Bridget had glanced over her shoulder to look out through
the window.

'That's the girl who is likely to have an accident, it's always
the ones that don't listen.'

His blistering tone guillotined her last trace of interest and
I knew that one child, at least, would never go on the
trampoline. The harangue continued for a little longer, and
then he must have sensed our collective depression, for he
clapped his hands twice as if to dispel the gloomy polter-
geists that he had released.

'Now then, who is going to volunteer first? Perhaps we
should give the ladies present first choice.'

The ladies present remained sitting and met his appeal with
a silent 'No'. The boys muttered a bit, but none of them
budged. I wondered whether I should give them a lead and
clamber on to the thing, but somehow I identified with their
rejection. None of the other teachers moved. There was an
awkward silence.

'Well, I'll be the first, as nobody seems to be interested.'

Mr Zip leapt up on to the trampoline and explained the
processes involved in jumping on to the net, then flying up
into the air, landing on your bottom and bouncing back on
to your feet. It certainly wasn't possible to do that anywhere
else without permanent injury. Everyone else must have been
curious, because we waited once more with some eagerness
for the forthcoming event. Maggie leaned over to me and
whispered,

'I wish he'd bounce off it.'

'Shut up,' I hissed.

His face never changed expression, even as he twirled and
twizzled in the air, and he finished the demonstration more
coldly formal than when he began it. For one moment I felt
he might salute, but there was no flag in sight. The children

offered more charity than the adults and a spontaneous round of applause greeted his final bounce. The warm reception thawed him out a bit; he smiled, click!

'Now then, who's going to be the first to try?'

There were no immediate offers, but I could see that Joe was straining like a greyhound in the traps.

'Go on then, Joe,' I said quietly.

He stood up, looked round and smiled. The smile made us responsible for the atmosphere and we gave him a cheer. After Joe had ventured into space, all of the children took their turn and the teachers present took over the encouragement. Mr Zip remained with us for safety. I say all of the children, but this is not quite true. Bridget, who was not normally reticent, resisted the charms of the trampoline and we all knew why; nobody bothered to cajole her overmuch, it was quite obvious that we could not heal her resentment there and then and, in all fairness, her feelings were not unjustified.

Maggie thanked the trampoline instructor politely and formally and we ambled out as another group filed in. As we were passing the window I could overhear the same sermon being delivered to the newly arrived cohort. The children had begun to run across the wide expanse of grass. One or two were hanging on to the arms of the adults and in this setting it was easy to see that instruction had little to do with teaching, that skills needed to be shared, not shown, and any marriage between learner and teacher would end in a bill of divorce if these simple facts were not adhered to.

We visitors left at 6 pm that evening. The sky had darkened and the wind carried some fine rain – or it could have been spray from the sea. There was to be a concert that night and our children were rehearsing songs and dances. Kathy (one of the mums) was doing some washing and Maggie (looking rather tired) was sewing a torn raincoat. We left quietly and none of us spoke much on the way back to London. I had enjoyed the visit, but it was not possible in such a short space of time to be part of the completeness of that holiday or any such holiday. One could only hope to eavesdrop and glean a little and that's what we had done.

It is difficult to support Shaw's dictum: 'He who can, does. He who cannot, teaches.' Teachers, or at least the ones I have known, remind one of the sea, where vast quantities of untapped wealth lie hidden or unrecognised. Like the sea, teachers are variable and subject to change, but the resources are there and need to be sought and used. If Maggie Gates was representative of the North Sea, then Sheelagh Pope could be cast in a more temperate zone – say the Mediterranean.

She had spent most of her twenty-six years in Cornwall, before coming to London at eighteen to train as an actress. It was a Catholic girlhood.

'The nuns were horrified that I painted my nails; and my hair (which is one of the good things about me) was cut short. I had to stay at the convent some weekends if Mummy was working away from home. I shall never forget it, because the nuns always woke us by sprinkling holy water over our faces. Honestly, first thing in the morning, water is water, it really made me shudder.'

In spite of the water, she remained a Catholic, a good one too, always far more concerned with charity than with sin. Physically she was stunning. Tall, but with an ample figure usually covered in flowing clothes, large green eyes and a pale complexion that sheltered under long copper-coloured hair which fell to her shoulders. Any compliments offered her about her appearance were flatly rejected.

'Oh, no, my arms are awful, you know when I'm walking down the street quite suddenly, without warning. I feel I'm fat. I suppose it's wrong to worry about it really.'

If ever we had visitors in school, the men usually wanted to return to her room when I mentioned that they might want to re-visit any classroom which was of special interest to them.

There was always something of interest going on in her room, she was a most prepared and painstaking teacher, but I do feel that some of the visitors returned to Room 5 for reasons other than observing educational method and teaching. The deep husky voice and striking appearance were never short of an audience. It was the legitimate theatre's loss.

I have mentioned the importance of timing in teaching: it is perhaps even more important as far as teacher/head teacher relationships are concerned. I made one of my worst mistakes one morning as I entered Sheelagh's room. The first hour of the day had been riddled with demands of one kind or another and the heating had failed in two of the classrooms. In spite of this fractious start, I should have known better.

'Ship – it sails on the sea. I will say the word again because I think some of you were not listening too well: sh-sh-ship, got it?'

Sheelagh was attempting a formal spelling lesson. I would not condemn it except that, at the particular time, the group was too large and the range of ability too wide for the method involved.

I went over to her desk and gave her a thank-you note from one of the mothers (Sheelagh had mended some torn trousers for her).

'I think spelling wheels would be better if you are doing spelling with such a large group. You will meet all their individual needs this way, the teaching and progression will be much easier for you and them.'

Sheelagh rose from her desk and seemed to tower above me. I had been pernickety and I knew it. Lady Macbeth stood before me, composed, cold and still.

'Oh, do you?'

This was all she said, all she needed to say. I left the room. An hour later I sent her a note apologising and at break-time she came to me.

'I was going to come to you, you were quite right.'

I did not accept her generosity. I could have easily waited two days before suggesting an alternative approach, and even then I could have introduced the issue without hurting anyone's feelings. This incident never marred our working relationship but similar ones, unless patched up quickly, must cause endless trouble and concern in schools everywhere.

In the autumn of that year, she asked to see me privately. 'Tom, I think I should let you know that I am returning to Cornwall, it's not that I want to leave, I don't and the . . .'

I didn't let her finish.

'I know you do, you're in love with someone down there, aren't you?'

She smiled very slowly: 'I don't know whether it will work out, and I will stay for the whole year if you want me to, I don't want the children to suffer on my account.'

'I think you should go if you feel you must and I don't think you should wait a year. Do you think you could?'

She looked at the floor and said, 'No, I don't, but I'm not sure.'

'If you go, then you'll know, won't you?'

'Yes, I suppose so.'

She left at the end of that term and sent us letters and cards glowing with descriptions of the Cornish landscape – the world was all sea, sky, rugged cliffs and daffodils. I always felt there was a bit more to it all than that and have always preferred people to places. It seemed Sheelagh was of the same opinion, for within three months she had decided not to stay there, not to teach in Paris, but to return to us. She is still making her way through the skyscraper blocks and shabby grey terraces of East London, not very different from many young teachers today, vulnerable, but assured and caring deeply for the poor. I never knew what happened or what went right or wrong in Cornwall. Since she has come back, she is an even better teacher than before.

9

MY HAIR IS CURLY, MY SKIN IS BROWN

The portraits of Maggie Gates and Sheelagh Pope present completely different images in both style and personality; in a sense, their differences enhance them. Team teaching was never thrust upon people, but it grew gradually and all of us benefitted.

'Tom, do you mind if I join Maggie with my girls for games? I have about seven or eight who really don't like netball and it's just cruel to push or persuade them into it. Maggie agrees because she has roughly the same number in this category. I thought perhaps I could do some individual games with them and some country dancing.'

'Can I take all my group in to Paul this week – we are making a witches' house out of cardboard boxes and things and it would be nice if we could work together, he's so clever . . .'

'I wonder if Steve and I could join together for this TV programme on travel? He can do the questioning and I can make out the questionnaires and charts . . .'

In this way, teaching strengths were built on and weaknesses were lessened rather than emphasised.

It gave most of the staff an opportunity to meet and see all the children. No child was ever 'pecked' to death in the staffroom by a failed teacher, although teachers naturally found that some children gave them less strain than others.

'Oh, I don't mind him too much, he gets a bit much around home-time, but he never worries me.'

'I can't think how you stand it.'

'Well, I'd rather have a hundred of him than one Lorraine, she exhausts me, it's just one demand after another . . .'

A deep and abiding mutual respect grew over a period of three years and within that span of time, our working community became both supportive and protective. Teachers are often asked to describe children, but a reversal of this situation is not called for in many schools. It is a pity; children can give adults a sharp jolt as to how they are seen through the eyes of a child. Our school magazine presented us with the following information about ourselves without fuss or verbal clutter.

Teacher Quiz
Here is a list of names to help you guess who the quiz is about: Mrs Gates, Mr Wakefield, Mrs Macpherson, Miss King, Mrs Watkins, Miss Pope, Mrs Harding, Miss Reid, Mrs Perraudin, Mr Howitt, Mr Hallum, Mr Baker, Mr Joyce, Mrs East.

1 This teacher is a lady and she has red-gold hair and she is in Class 4. She wears midis, rings and bracelets and sometimes earrings and scarves. She never has her hair up and she always comes to school looking nice. Her voice is deep and soft and she wears make-up. She is very nice and wears boots. Her class bring books home to read. She wears a red rain mac and her favourite colour is red, I think. Who is it?

2 This man helps me with my work and he lets me do lots of work. Sometimes I like him and sometimes I don't like him, but he does let us play games sometimes. He has pink skin and brown hair and green eyes. He wears a brown suit and a brown tie and a white shirt. He got married this year and he is very happy. His wife is happy he likes her a lot. She is having a baby. He is very nice to her and he is my teacher. He buys her lots of things. He takes us for school sports and on outings . . .

3 This teacher is quite good at cooking and good at cake mixtures. The children like her because she teaches them to cook and they take home cooking. She was at the zoo with us and she was quite good to the boys and girls. She looks like

a cookery lady and her hair is white and her cookery coat is blue. She sits in the staffroom crocheting and she takes only ten children and she goes home at half-past four. She likes cookery and she prepares the lessons well . . .

4 This teacher is a woodwork and craft teacher. He takes us on a Friday to woodwork He is a good teacher. He came from Australia but he has been in Canada. I like it when we use the machines. I made a game and although I am a girl, I like doing metalwork. We went over to the park to fly a kite today. There was no wind, but there was sun and we came back disappointed. He has long hair and he wears modern clothes. He wears a brown shirt and a white tie sometimes. I like doing enamelling. I made a pendant this year . . .

5 This teacher helps us with our music. He helps me to play the piano and he plays the guitar and piano in assembly. He can play instruments and teaches us songs in the assembly. I think he is very shy because he is quiet except when he sings or plays. I think he is a good teacher. He is very clever. His hair is yellowish . . .

6 This teacher helps me at school. She is kind to me as I am big and sometimes we are naughty and this teacher is unhappy. Sometimes we are very good, then this teacher is happy. She helps us to measure and count. I like reading to this teacher and she helps me to write in my book. This teacher gives us paper and paints and we are making things for the school. She takes us for rounders and netball and painting and art. She wears round glasses and scarves. Her hair is greyish and her face is pink . . .

It would be foolish to be paternalistic with children who were capable of such observation, and unjust of us if we had not let them take part in decision-making within our school. Retardation evidently did not impair integrity or truthfulness, nor did it make them insensitive to the needs of others. School rules were few in number if one could count them as rules. The children were asked about uniforms and, like the staff, they did not like the idea very much. There were rules on safety which, when presented carefully, they accepted.

'I want you to put both hands over your eyes – yes, all of

you. Keep them there, let's see if you can keep them there for one minute. It seems a very long time doesn't it? I wonder what it's like not to be able to see at all? Throwing stones in the playground could blind any of us, how would you feel if you threw a stone, not at anybody, just playing and you hit Andrew (point to small child) and then he wouldn't be able to see any more?'

Older girls would shake their heads in dismay and older boys agreed vociferously.

'Can we all agree then, never to do this?'

The dangers of racing around a school with twisting corridors and swing doors were similarly demonstrated and walking rather than running in the school building was accepted without acrimony. It was never a case of '*You* may not do this because . . .' but rather '*We* cannot do this, can *we*?' All staff were brought in on such discussions so that we were viewed together and not in isolation. Children recognise and react to harmony in adult relationships and I feel this easily recognisable factor helped greatly towards the stability of the school in all its aspects.

A lot has been written on cruelty to children and fact and fiction have embroidered the theme of children being cruel to other children. Little has been said of children's compassion, probably because outlets for this are never or rarely provided. One assembly revealed this compassion so clearly, it was more simple, more grave and more satisfying than any pieta. A film on air travel was to be shown to all the school in the afternoon and I felt I would prepare the children for the film, not 'over-sell' it, just ginger their interest a little. We talked about different kinds of air travel, such as aeroplanes, helicopters, and space rockets. We did little improvisations of work involved, like stewardessing, piloting, and safety controls. At the end of this, I had compiled fourteen huge flash cards of words to remember or words to listen for. I had graded them so that it was possible for all classes to recognise a word and hold it up for the rest of the school. Words like helicopter, aeroplane, danger, safety, landing, pilot and exit were placed in a Lotto arrangement on a huge table and volunteers from every class came out and selected the word as I called the name out. Then they held it up and received their due applause. This exercise was clearly beyond the reception class of five-year-olds and, although they enjoyed clapping, I felt sad that they were excluded. Within a few minutes, thirteen children, looking like an advertisement for UNICEF, were gleefully standing in a row holding the flash cards. There was one left on the table. It was impossible for any child to make a mistake in selecting the right one. I glanced at the reception class and noticed David, in spite of his cumbersome harness which was worn to correct a spinal deformity, was sitting there giving everything all the attention he could muster.

'David Willington, would you like to find the word "balloon" for me please.'

He scrambled on to the stage with some difficulty, but certainly no lack of dignity. He placed both hands on the table and studied the single word in front of him as though it were alive. He frowned as some of the other children had done when they were making a choice. I was apprehensive in case some of the children might laugh at, or deride, the situation. The hall was silent. David stretched forward, took the card in his hand and shouted triumphantly,

'Balloon, balloon, this says balloon.'

At break-time, one of the teachers asked about the heavy applause session, as she had heard the clapping in the stockroom.

'Oh, it was David Willington guessing the right word.'

'Is that all that noise was about?'

'No, not quite.'

The barriers of the school as an establishment apart from parents had slowly been eroded by our meetings and attitudes. One of our major problems was the difficulty in seeing both parents together. If Mum came along, then Dad had to look after the children; it was not often that both parents could relax and meet us together. One Christmas we overcame this by offering to babysit for parents who were interested in a theatre outing to the West End. Half the staff elected to enter-tain the children at school, whilst the rest of us accompanied the parent on a visit to a show of their choice 'up West'. Of the thirty or so parents who were going on the trip, over half had never been to a theatre in their life before and a quarter had never visited the West End of London. Fares and home pressures would castrate any hopes of ever achieving this. We left the choice of show to them. We were quite prepared to book for Covent Garden if they so wished. As it turned out they preferred a visit to Danny La Rue at the Palace Theatre.

The mini-coach, which the Variety Club of Great Britain had kindly loaned us, arrived promptly – we left later than scheduled, as we had to sort out tea and games for the children in school and inevitably one or two parents were late because of minor hazards of everyday family life. No sooner were we all packed into the coach than the sweets came out. Maltesers and chocolates were passed this way and that and a generous father had brought along a bottle of sherry for good measure. By the time we reached Leicester Square, I was feeling very happy but slightly sick. An autocratic car attendant forbade us parking space and the driver was ready to return in despair. This wouldn't do at all. I got out and began to argue with the attendant and was soon joined by four huge West Indians. Within a surprisingly short time, he appeared to agree with the justice of our case and eventually let us park on his limousine-sanctified ground. The theatre itself did not inhibit us. We were the noisiest group in the upper circle and choco-lates were still being gulped down before the show started. Mrs Levenson's box of assorteds cascaded over the safety rail, showering the stalls with cellophane-wrapped bits of goodwill.

I don't know whether they enjoyed the occasion or the show most. Returning home, the excitement and fun of it all hadn't abated. Just as we were climbing out of the coach, I spoke to Mr Allan.

'Did you enjoy it, Mr Allan?'

'Yes, I have a great time, thanks, work tomorrow though.'

'It's the same for all of us. Where was Mrs Allan sitting? I didn't see her.'

'Oh, she not come, she stay at school with the kids and Mrs Harding and the other teachers. I take my mate with me instead, she's not one for going out.'

I didn't pursue the issue further, but felt a mild sense of defeat. We are seeing a change in attitude towards the individual rights of women and I hope that these rights will extend to mothers who sacrifice not only their youth, but their lives, in maintaining their families and often receive less than a gesture of acknowledgement for doing it. For many mothers that I know, their families do not constitute a fulfilment of themselves, but an emotional sanction which places their own personal hopes, ambitions and needs in abeyance for a very long time, if not for ever.

This kind of experience with parents emphasised the importance of visits out of the school building, as well as the need to eradicate the idea that a school should be an oyster bed with the pearls firmly protected and enclosed behind tight shells. The school leavers were asked to take part in all kinds of visits, at both a cultural and a working level. They visited in groups and also alone. On one occasion, after a visit to a hairdressing exhibition, Evelyn telephoned.

'Oh, is that you Sir, it's me, Evelyn, me and Doreen are lost. We are on the tube and we followed the right colours and we should be in King's Cross, but we're not. Don't worry' – she began to laugh – 'it's OK, the station man is putting us right. He's been very good about it. He's black, this place we're at is called Oval I think. We'll be back late though.'

'All right Evelyn, I'll wait here for you and I'll let your mums know that you'll be a bit late home from school.'

'See you then, Sir; can't say much more 'cos the money is running out of the machine. We won't be long, it's club tonight and I don't want to be late. Is Herbert in school today?'

'Yes, he is.'

'Can you tell him Jeanette found his football socks and she's taken them to the launderette with the other stuff, see you later.'

Visitors to the school were of as much interest to us as we were to them. I had worked in other schools where visitors were escorted round and peered at children as though they were in a goldfish bowl. If people came to see us, they were encouraged to sit and talk to the children, not just stare. In turn, the children talked and asked questions back, thus sparing adult and child from an asinine exercise. This conversation could well have taken place between a child and a visitor.

'What's your name? Have you come here before?'

'Mrs Freeman, what's yours? Yes, I saw you in the play at Christmas.'

'Oh did you? I'm Alfred. There's fluff all over your jumper, it's not fur is it? My cat's fur comes off and my mum has to brush it off our clothes.'

'No, it's special wool. It's called angora, it's fluffy wool. I like your picture, is that your sister you have drawn?'

'No.' (A pause as Alfred continues painting. He looks up.) 'Why have you come here, are you Andrew's mum?'

'No, I'm a school governor, I'm interested in what you do. I like this school and I want to help as much as I can.'

'Oh, are you married? What does your husband do?'

'He's a doctor.'

'My dad works on the tube, he works all night sometimes. Is your doctor-husband black or white?'

'He's black.'

'So's mine and my mum is half and half.'

'She's just like my children then.'

'Oh.'

School governors are almost always presented as cardboard busybodies. I never found this borne out in my experience. Our group of fifteen or so was constituted from parents, teachers, the local authority and allied professional or interested groups. Their visits were never relegated to special occasions nor related to their personal self-esteem and, since every day should be a prize-day for a child in some way, so we were spared the unctuous platitudes of a prize-day by its abolition. It might sound lame, but I genuinely believe that all the governors were concerned for the welfare of the school, and all of them supported us however they were best able. Our chairman, Mrs Mair Garside, was also an active politician. She looked like everybody's mother, roly-poly, warm and friendly. Yet, there was a questioning directness behind the maternal charms which had to be met rather than assuaged. The staff came to like her greatly. She would often leave her bag or scarf somewhere which made it difficult for her ever to say goodbye, because she was always coming back for something she had left. I had always hoped that she might become an MP sometime. Parliament could do with people like her but, as one parent said, 'Well, how can she be an MP, she talks straight don't she, she tells the truth.'

The remark was typical of an underlying feeling that politics was something apart from their lives, and most of the parents viewed all politicians sceptically. However, in the case of Mair Garside, I'm sure that, like me, most of them would vote for her if ever the chance were given. I hope it is, some day.

Other visitors gave less cause for rapture. Each term we decided on a quota, as too many people visiting from several linked professional areas could have swamped us as far as our work with the children was concerned. There were teachers in training, nurses, doctors, the press, social workers, community relations officers and visitors from overseas. What pleased me most was watching their curiosity change to a sense of wonder after they had met and talked to the children. At times, their questions were met with an irritable response from me. It depended often on my own fatigue how I handled it all.

'There doesn't seem anything wrong with many of them, and they all look so happy; and they look perfectly normal,' said a green-tweed visitor.

'There's no reason why they shouldn't look perfectly normal, or why they shouldn't be happy and normal (whatever that is) anyway. They are here because they are 'educationally' sub-normal. Would you like me to define the term? I will, but you must accept that I reject it myself on the grounds that educational normality has never been truly defined to me.'

My answer lacked objectivity, but the truth of it must have been felt. This kind of conversation often took place. I never felt that any child in our school did not require specialised help, but the adjective 'sub-normal' I found difficult to get through my teeth.

Reading ability, learning skills, as well as any industrial training must be stultified in children who were given little opportunity, or who had never had any knowledge or experience of their own creativity. Did some visitors expect to see bovine groups of listless children ploughing their way through endless basketry or perpetually threading beads. On referral, little was ever said about individual creative urges or abilities. You might get 'He draws well' or 'She enjoys singing', but no satisfactory tests have been concocted to ascertain creativity and I am sure that many so-called 'break-throughs' in teaching methods are merely the tapping and releasing of this still largely unknown human force.

What presents me with the largest ache is the total urban schooling situation. At present, we are living in huge, man-made concrete-plastic conurbations and 90 per cent of us have had little say in the growth of the environment which surrounds us. Most of our creativity is being squashed or buried by an environment which we have had little or no part in building. Before the school opened, I trudged and squelched through mud and sludge and toured the building with a grumbling works foreman. The building had given him headaches, its design was not of the 'traditional' pattern. It did not look like a giant shoe-box with windows. Consequently, its construction had caused endless difficulties. The original architect had been sacked or had left with some ill-will and the finishing touches of the building were left in the hands of another architect who demonstrated little enthusiasm for the project. The whole area was devastated by clearance, but the back of the school opened on to green playing fields. The front presented a different picture. The entrance looked out on to a vista of piled rubble and half-demolished Victorian houses, which exposed whole rooms and ruptured staircases to the public gaze. Small bonfires of burning waste dotted between the houses gave notice that the onslaught was continuous.

There, in the middle of all this, was a building which might have looked more at home in Nazareth or Jerusalem than in London. Its appearance was undoubtedly Eastern; grey salt-stone blocks were capped with perspex bubbles which rose to the sky on twelve versions of a western European minaret. I managed to see the original architect. I liked his building and it was important for me to tell him so. When we met, he explained how he felt the building could be utilised and clearly, although the finished piece was unorthodox, it remained intimate, functional and attractive and, what is more, the children enjoyed it. Within a four-year period, damage of any kind to the building was very slender indeed. At the end of this period, the Victorian ghost houses had all been replaced by soaring tower-blocks, which reared over us in the most strident fashion. Our minarets withstood their shadows with equally strident individuality. The comparison between the two developments always puts me in mind of the 'Tom and Jerry' cartoons.

In most primary and special schools, however idyllic the building, one is always confronted with problems of space. A generous staffing allowance can do little to help in this problem and even the most careful timetabling does not nearly eliminate the restrictions and hazards in loss of time placed on teaching when a school is being run at capacity-roll level. Our hall was an assembly hall, a dining-room for 160 children each day, a gymnasium and a dance centre, as well as a theatre. Utilising it to the full and meeting all these needs was not easy – yet we managed. Jeremy Baker, our music teacher, suffered most. I never heard him complain as he pursued guitar lessons, choir, music and movement, infant percussion groups, through endless interruptions as chairs and tables were moved or gymnasium apparatus was stored away. I think his Quaker background must have maintained his equilibrium because attempting to teach music in a partitioned section of the hall must have been nightmarish at times. All the staff worried for him, but none could come up with an idea that might ease his situation. Finally it was eased and children solved it, creatively, actively, without any motives except concern for the particular teacher and a real appreciation of the subject that he was teaching them.

'Stop pushing Merva, go on, you tell him.'

'I'm not, you tell him Maureen, it's your idea.'

'Is he in there? I think he's in the staffroom. I'll tell him tomorrow.'

'No, tell him now, go on . . .'

It was five o'clock and record club had ended. I was sitting stewing over some recent referrals to the school and, as usual, was wondering how far all the forms, tests, reports, correlated with the flesh and blood they represented. These bits of teen-age conversation interspersed with giggles spilled through the open door of my secretary's room and I was enjoying my unintentional eavesdropping. I didn't want to keep myself in suspense any longer. If it was an argument arising from the record club dance, then I would prefer it settled now.

I opened the door and said, 'Did you want me, girls?'

Shirley nodded, smiling as she did so. I noticed that on her shiny brown nose little bubbles of perspiration had formed. From the look on all the faces of the girls, the bubbles were due to the demands of the recent reggae and not caused by any argument or discontent. These girls would be leaving soon and looking at them, one could not but notice the attractive and individual style of their clothes. Instead of muted tones and matching twinsets, they wore colours that clashed like a visual gong. Lime green jumpers and red checked skirts or multi-flowered skirts with lightning-flash tops enhanced their appearance. It was part of them, just as their singing and dancing was. Like so many West Indian children themselves, the effect was volatile but truthful.

'Sir, can you come with us for a minute?'

'Are you asking me for a dance, Shirley? I've been waiting so long for this moment.'

They laughed.

'No, it's serious, isn't it Maureen?'

Maureen nodded in assent. I followed them into the hall and noticed Jeremy Baker locking up the record player – he always moved quietly. The girls waited until he had left the hall before they spoke.

'Sir, it's terrible for Mr Baker in the hall doing music, other kids or people are always spoiling things we start doing.'

'I know it is, Shirley, but it's not as easy . . .'

'He doesn't have to stay in the hall now, we've found another room for him.'

I stared blankly, as there was not an ounce of space left in the building.

'Come and look.'

I thought it might be a joke, but let them usher me along.

'Come and look.' Shirley opened the double doors which led into the dining table storage space. I was looking into a long narrow room; chairs had been arranged in a semicircular pattern and it could comfortably seat fifteen children with more than adequate space for movement. Before I could speak, the girls stated their case. Any giggles which were a front for shyness had now disappeared.

'There ain't any windows – but look there is plenty of light from that.' Shirley pointed to the roof which was topped by one of the plastic minarets.

'But what about ventilation Shirley – air to breathe?'

'We thought of that, you can have round holes cut into that plastic that have wheels in that whizz round.'

'Yes, you can, we have one in our bathroom and the gas people put one in the kitchen when we were converged,' said Merva.

'Converged?'

'Oh, you know what I mean.'

I did, so I shut up and listened more.

'Mrs Whatser-name – Garside, she'll get us a fan if you ask her, won't she? Anyway, we might not need one.'

'We can leave the tables where they are now (the dining recess). We just stacked them a bit higher and the cooks say it's less trouble for them in getting the tables out and ready for lunch.'

Their argument was unassailable. I didn't want to quarrel with it and they could see that I was pleased. By 10 am the next morning we had a music-room. Since then it has always retained a special quality for me, even when it is empty of children, I look at the pictures on the wall and the array of medlodicas, xylophones and self-made maraccas as though they were an appetising meal. What a luxury it all seems, there must be more to come from the same direction. The awareness is there, all it needs is a chance. Babies are born with a creative instinct, but what happens to it? What agencies are responsible for its repression or death? Is it family, schooling as we know it now, work pressures, values? I don't know. I do know it's there and I am sure that it is more important than intellect. I have seen it in adolescents (as recorded) and in very young children. The following observations were made by an infants teacher that I am fortunate enough to know. I have worked with her in several schools and the clarity of her notes will give some indication of the basis of my admiration for her.

Loretta, aged 5. Physical handicap, sickle cell anaemia, causing much lethargy.

When she first came to school, Loretta was a timid, withdrawn little girl who was afraid to make any decisions at all. She used to ask what she should do in a quiet, almost inaudible voice and need constant reassurance. At first, I would offer her the choice of two activities because I felt that she could not cope with more freedom. Gradually she began to take more responsibility and, by the end of the year, was using her freedom wisely. Her concentration has improved, but she is a child who, due to her handicap, sometimes feels very tired and appears lethargic. If I saw that was the case, I would ask her if she would like to lie down and, on occasion, she has slept for long periods. Sometimes, when she has awakened and has chosen an activity to pursue, I have asked one of my assistants to sit with her and to work with her because, in addition to the fact that this has developed her co-operation, I also had to remember that Loretta was too tired to make very much effort. I believe that when working with children one must be careful not to impose one's own ideas, and a creative product must contain as much of the child as possible, but, in the case of physically handicapped, sometimes by the very nature of their handicap it would be impossible for them to work quickly enough to finish a piece of work before becoming bored with it. I think that all small children need to see the result of their work as quickly as possible, because they have not yet developed the patience to wait for any long-term activity to be completed, and they enjoy immediate satisfaction. Therefore, in the case of Loretta, I have not felt it 'cheating' if either of my assistants has helped in the creation of a picture or a model, because they are both sensitive enough to know how much help to give and to allow Loretta to make as much contribution to the activity as possible. During the year she developed enough confidence to volunteer pieces of information about her family, which seems to be a happy one, and she began to draw pictures of her brother, first with no body, but gradually developing until, by the end of the year, her pictures were showing quite a lot of detail. Her observation improved very much and she used to help me to tidy the classroom, remembering the places in the cupboard for our equipment. Her power of reasoning developed and if anything was lost, she would look in the most likely places for it first before saying to herself 'Now, where could it be?' if she could not find it. Often she has found a missing object by reasoning out where to look for it. I believe that creative activity has helped Loretta to develop her thinking, in addition to giving her the confidence to choose an activity and to use her freedom well.

John, aged 5. Physical handicap, spina bifida.

John was beginning to enjoy coming to school, after a very apprehensive start, when he had to go into hospital for a long period. I wondered if this experience would upset him, but when he came back to school he began to develop very well. He has always enjoyed painting and drawing, and from the beginning has been an observant child. I found that with physically handicapped children, it is sometimes necessary to draw their attention to details and thus help them to develop their observation, but with John, this has not been necessary. His paintings and drawings contain minute details and have always been very lively. When I went into school recently, the class had made a frieze and included in this frieze was a figure, which John had made, using paints and waste materials, representing his father. He had captured his father's expression exactly, and it was quite amazing to see the likeness. He has one particular friend, Neil, with whom he loves especially to play, though he is a sociable child and interested in all the children. He and Neil often put on hats, and take a toy driving-wheel to sit under a shelf in the classroom pretending to drive to the seaside. In fact, this is a favourite activity of many of the children and sometimes they would nearly all be found sitting in a row under the shelf driving away some-where. This helped to develop their imagination and we would have long conversations about where they were going, what they would do when they reached their destination, how many cars and lorries were on the road, and what they would have to eat when they arrived. John's favourite dish was fish and chips. Often the destination would be the seaside and fortunately we always had sand and water available in the classroom. To develop the game further, John liked to make cakes and pies with the sand and sometimes, at this point, the game would take another direction because his imagination might lead him to remark,

'Shall we have a birthday party with these cakes and pies? Whose birthday is it? It can be Neil's and he is five.'

He would look for five sticks to push into the 'cake' as candles and we would sing 'Happy Birthday' to Neil. I think that games such as these are very helpful, particularly to physically handicapped children, because when they are at home they do not have as much opportunity for communi-cation with others in their play as children who are able easily to go out together, to play in the garden or the nearest park. I feel that John's imagination has helped to stimulate that of other children, who have eagerly joined in games, and often conversations, paintings, models have all been the result of this stimulation. I think that John has gained much confi-dence, become friendly and co-operative, largely as a result of creative activity. He is interested in what he does and I consider that if children in the reception class are interested, then a good basis for their education has been formed.

It seems that these children will not only act creatively if given the chance, but think creatively. That is why, although they are totally unaware of the existence of my music-room, it being several miles away from them, for me they are directly related and they represent its very existence. This ability to think and talk manifested itself during improvised play situations that I conducted with school leavers. To begin with, the improvisations were sheer entertainment value. One of the lessons went like this.

'Look, I want us to be a television audience for this afternoon. The cameras and recording crew are coming to this school and there is this fella who is going to ask some of you to tell the audience a bit about your lives. You've left school for five years and you have just come back to say hello, but remember you are on television. Cindy pull the blinds down, arrange your chairs in a semicircle. I will do the announcing, you know, like David Frost does, and nod if you want to be called for interview. Oh, I want a lighting engineer. All the lights must be off until I give the signal with my hand, then turn the top switch and light up this desk as though it were a screen.'

David's hand was lifted.

'Can I be 'im? I can mend motorbikes, but I don't like talkin'. Shall I stand here by the switch?'

I accepted his offer, it was most generous of him. He had already fixed himself up with a job as a garage mechanic and petrol fumes were sea breezes to him. I sat behind the desk in the darkened room.

'You ready, David?'

He nodded. I gave the signal and the desk was spotlighted.

'Ah, good afternoon, ladies and gentlemen. This afternoon we are bringing you a special TV programme called "Going Back". Here today we have prominent people visiting their old school. The studio audience is here with us and already you can hear the applause. (It came, and I knew that the audience was captive.) I can see there is someone making her way up here right now, it's a very attractive young lady. Stavroulla will be here in just two seconds. (More clapping as Stavroulla moves herself into our television screen.) Ah, good afternoon, it's so good to see you here again, Stavroulla. How have you been these last five years, I wonder if you would like to tell us something about them?'

'Well, er (she giggles) I can't tell you everyfink, some of it's private.' (All class laugh.)

'Well keep the private bits to yourself then and tell us the rest.'

'Oh, I've been ever so busy. When I left here I was a trained cutter and machinist and I got a job wiv my uncle's cousin, he's from Cyprus as well, but he's not my cousin. Least, I don't fink he is. There was this other Greek boy there and he wanted me to be engaged, but I weren't interested. My uncle he makes clothes, no, costumes for shows. You know, the Talk of the Town, London Palladium and all that and TV. There's always feathers and sparkling buttons all over everywhere at the factory, it's only little, but I like it, we have to work ever so quick. Anyway my uncle, sorry my cousin's uncle, he takes me along to the theatre now and I help 'im with the fittin' as well as doing some of the cuttin'. Next April he says I can travel with a show all over America, and I have to look after all the costumes and clothes. The money's good and I think it will be exciting.'

'I expect you are looking forward to your trip to the USA. Which part do you want to visit most?'

'Oh, it's not sure I'm going yet, there's this boy in Cyprus who wants to marry me. I have to think about it, but I'll let you know what I do.'

'Thank you so much for coming along, I'm sure the studio audience have loved seeing you again.'

'Oh, don't say that, it's been a pleasure – 'bye, folks.'

'Now we have a young man making his way through the audience.' (There were some cheers for Michael, not given for the role he was playing, more likely on account of his quiet manner and tolerance that he accorded to almost everyone at all times.)

'Good afternoon, sir.'

'Afternoon, nice to be back, how are you?'

'Well that's just what we wanted to ask you.'

'Oh, I'm fine, still in the same job, got a rise last week as well. They are putting me into another group, it sets up central heating in houses, the contacts come through the gas board. We have to work in a team and there are five in my group. They're a good lot of blokes and I get on with them OK. 'Course I'm only learnin' at the moment, but it's not too hard. One of the blokes is my mate most.'

'Oh, is he your age?'

'No, he's old, I should think he's about forty. The others take the rise out of him sometimes 'cos of his roll-up fags. Cor, they don't half make a stink. When he gets his tin and fag papers out everybody disappears, it puts you off your sandwiches. He's very good to me though, I've been to his home, he's got two sons older than me and he's showing me how to do pipe fitting and I can use his workshop any time – yes, he's a good old bloke.'

'He's not that old, Michael.'

'Yes, he is, do you know he puts ear plugs in when his sons have "Top of the Pops" on. I'm not too keen on one of the blokes at work, but I steer clear of him most of the time. He's a real trouble-maker, always tryin' to cause arguments and he goes on and on about the Irish and nig-nogs and blacks and all that stuff. Like Alf Garnett does, but it's not funny, it's real nasty. I'm half Irish and sometimes I feel like saying something, but Harry (that's my old mate) usually shuts him up.'

'You are enjoying your work then?'

'Oh, yes, you get tired though you know, I have to be up at seven in the morning and we only get half an hour for dinner, it's not like school, you know. Yes, I do enjoy it, I buy my own clothes now, help my Mum out a bit and save a bit. My sister's getting engaged and when she's married she and her boyfriend are moving out of London. I think I'll stay with them some of the time. I might move out later on and see how it goes. See you again then, cheerio.'

I suppose to many teenagers a forty-year-old must seem to be verging on dotage, but this 'interview' effectively demolishes the so-called generation gap. Michael had accepted the roll-ups as long as he didn't have to smoke them and Harry had reacted similarly to "Top of the Pops". Both had rejected social attitudes which were clearly abhorrent to them and, in spite of their differences in interests and leisure, their working relationship was based on friendship and respect for one another.

The commercial world was brought into our programme. It was suggested by the children and expression of their opinions of it was not diluted. Children are not easily fooled; as advertising techniques become more subtle, then consumers become more cautious or even cynical. I've often used actual hire purchase advertisements to show that certain commodities are not really being 'given away' and that the 'free gift' advertisement usually means a contract entailing debt.

'Sir, can we put some adverts in between like they do on ITV, we can have a laugh then?'

'All right, split into three groups and we can shove them in after each interview. I'll give five minutes.'

The three groups were whispering and laughing. It was like watching three separate joyful plots; there was little argument and roles were adopted rather than cast. They were all well-prepared before the proposed time-limit and the results were uproariously funny as well as being shrewd in observation. One in particular left us all exhausted with mirth.

Jennifer tripped blithely through woodland haunts of leaf and fern, stooped and drank the cold water of a mountain stream, sniffed and swooned over the scent of numerous flowers before lowering herself on to a handy fallen tree in what seemed to be a catatonic trance. She sat and wistfully ran her fingers through imaginary windswept hair. (Enter Herbert slapping his thighs.)

'What's he walking like that for?' whispered Helen.

'Sh, sh, he's on a horse stupid, those blokes are always on horses.' Our hero dismounted with the panache of an Olympian god. He produced the inevitable packet of cigarettes that would unite this modern Juno and Jupiter for ever. Alas, catastrophe was not beyond these fair immortals and the cigarette failed to unite them. They coughed and spluttered after the first two imaginary whiffs and puffs of the magical weed. Romance was thwarted by a cloud of smoke and choking spasms. The surrounding foliage caught fire as the fatal cigarettes were discarded in the face of true love and Juno and Jupiter ran in opposite directions to escape the ensuing tobacco flames of passion that they had inspired.

'You never know what might happen if you smoke – cigarettes!'

There was a lovely all-girl advertisement which took place at the hairdresser's. One of the West Indian girls had decided to have her hair 'straightened' and was understandably annoyed when she saw the black strong halo that surrounded her lovely brown face transformed into dead, lank tresses. She complained bitterly and the attending hairdresser poured vitriol on the situation when she suggested that the stricken customer might want her skin 'lightened' to match the nightmare coiffure.

'What you want, make me into a ghost? My hair is curly, my skin is brown. I am Hyacinth, that's me. You just get that cooking machine started. I want my hair the way it was. Nobody want to look at me if I look like that, I don't want to look at myself, that's not me anyway. I am Hyacinth.'

The interviews developed into job applications and interviews and roles became interchangeable. The employee became the employer. These improvisations, like many other forms of self-expression, heightened confidence and strengthened many self-images that had been damaged or weakened. Hyacinth's statement about herself bore no apology for her colour, in fact, it revealed quite the opposite and her validity as far as being young, gifted and black goes holds no doubts for me. One of the most exciting aspects of a multi-racial school, or a multi-racial society, for that matter, is the differing types of creativity different groups can offer. The total result is so vital that one must conclude that it is impossible to achieve a rich harmony without the differences.

As far back as 1962, Getzels and Jackson* came to the following conclusions on the group that they had identified as creative thinkers. Compared with other children they were:

1   Less concerned with scholastic success.
2   Less favoured by teachers.
3   Less apt to accept the teacher as a model to be copied.
4   Interested in a wider range of subjects.
5   Richer in their sense of humour.

The children that made up our school, although backward as far as basic subjects went, could bear out almost all of the five conclusions drawn by Getzels and Jackson.

* J. W. Getzels and P. W. Jackson. *Creativity and Intelligence* (Wiley, 1962).

10

THREE BOOS FOR THE HOLIDAYS

The bell of creation is ringing for ever,
The bell of creation is ringing for me.
Ring bell over the land, ring bell under the sea.
The bell of creation is ringing for ever,
And all of the time it is ringing for me.

A month before Christmas, our ding-donging set up such a
vibration that it left the staff totally wearied, yet becalmed
when it was all over. It was almost as though we had all
been exorcised or our emotions had undergone a great
purging. This particular song seemed to sum it all up. We discussed our Christmas plans and decided against the usual menu.

MENU

Hors d'oeuvre

Three Carols	1	O Little Town of Bethlehem
	2	Rocking Carol
	3	We Three Kings

Main Course

Nativity

Sweet or Pudding

Three More Carols	1	Hark the Herald Angels Sing
	2	Silent Night
	3	Away in a Manger

Cheese

Headmaster's Speech

The above menu is no attempt to belittle the ingredients. It's the presentation that so often causes the indigestion. The 'nativity', as far as stories go, still presents the best bill of fare. It has cruelty and power depicted in Herod and the judiciary of that time. Poverty is linked with both goodness and crime. We have magic, mysticism and wonder coupled with everyday life and ordinary people, and the birth itself is both simple and triumphant, but all this gets lost in Oxford Street at Christmas-time and the sparkle in schools ought to have a sounder basis than the neon lights. I don't think any of us wanted to pick up those artificial reflections.

Each class teacher had decided to do something 'different' and I left the choice of material to them. Out of eight classes, one teacher would always choose the 'nativity' and its simplicity and strength never failed to get through. Fortunately, we never had to use a doll as Jesus, real five-year-olds, black and poor, constituted far more than a substitute. Our Cypriot shepherds achieved an extraordinary realism without help from their ex-curtain via jumble sale Arab cloaks.

'Now remember, you've been working hard all day climbing hills, finding lost sheep, building pens, all kinds of things. It's the end of the day and you are all having a bit of peace around the fire. You can make up your own conversation. In the middle of your talking this shining angel appears. Are you ready? George, you jump on to the rostrum when I tell you.'

Darryl was talking to his class and I wondered what our three shepherds would talk about at the end of the day. It seemed rather a difficult improvisation to ask of them. The shepherds commenced their well-earned leisure like the crack from a starting pistol: to our astonishment they immediately began gambling. It was some kind of Greek dice game and for ten minutes or so the hillsides of Palestine had met the sea at Nicosia. Sheep were being won and lost as the dice were spilled on the ground and the inevitable arguments ensued, the noise growing louder as the quarrels intensified. George (our Gabriel) did not enter sloppily. If he had floated in, the shepherds wouldn't have been aware of his existence. He ran very fast the whole length of the hall and leapt on to the rostrum. The dice were scattered and, naturally enough, the shepherds expressed their fright in real terms.

'Oh, my God, what is it?'

'It's a ghost, it's a ghost, I'm goin', oh, what's all that light?'

'It's from the fire, stay where you are, this bloke's not come to hurt us, he's not carryin' a spear or anything like that, is he?'

'No, but what's he sparklin' for, I ain't never seen anybody sparklin' and glittering like that, and I don't like it and I'm going. The sheep can all jump in the lake as far as I'm concerned. I've had enough of this.'

Gabriel rescued the situation.

'Hold on a minute, don't be scared. I've got good news, not bad.'

The news was delivered simply and songs and carols were brought in when and where the children suggested they should be – and you can't stop West Indians dancing. These angels were not cut out for medieval composure and piety. They came forward swerving, gyrating and clapping.

> The Virgin Mary had a baby boy,
> The Virgin Mary had a baby boy,
> The Virgin Mary had a baby boy,
> And they said that His name was Jesus.
> Oh, yes believe us, Oh yes, believe us,
> And they said that His name was Jesus.

The line of singing and dancing celestials burst in and the success of this annual production was never in any doubt. It was their own interpretation of a timeless story and it was their freshness which gave it life.

The programme enveloped all kinds of plays, revues, stories and songs. *Androcles and the Lion* had broader philosophies and took on newer dimensions that even Shaw might have envied. Mageera (Androcles' wife) gave more than just cause for her complaints and did not emerge as a harridan. One of the infant classes presented a circus which would have challenged the ingenuity of any big top. The ringmaster in particular came into his own with his new-found managerial responsibility. The demanding, rather helpless child that we knew, was replaced by a ruthless official who commanded actors, clowns, lions and audience with continuous chat, cajolery and kindly orders.

'Ladies and gentlemen, l-a-d-i-e-s a-n-d g-e-n-t-l-e-m-e-n. (He boomed even louder.) L-a-d-i-e-s and gentlem-e-n. Now all of you, can't you hear me? When I start talking like this it means you stop and listen. Are you listening? Good. For our first act this afternoon we have Andy the weight-lifter, after that we have Lawrence who is an . . . We have Lawrence who is a . . . What are you again Lawrence? Yes, I forgot, he is an acrobat. You know, he swings upside down and back to front and everyfink like that, and we have clowns who make you laugh . . .'

It was soon clear to us all that without some kind of persuasion Robin our ringmaster was never going to leave the ring; the sawdust had clearly taken hold. Each announcement brought a fresh round of applause, but at the present rate of progress there would be no time left for the rest of the class to perform. Fortunately for the other members of the cast, Robin had begun to boss a section of the audience about in order to accommodate some late-comers.

'Come on, move along the row, they've paid to see this show, make more room, shove up . . . shift your arse, Missus.'

Poor Robin clamped his hand over his mouth, his face went beetroot red but, like the real trouper he had proved to be, he took a deep bow, lifted his top hat and marched off.

'Sorry Miss, I forgot.'

'You were very good Robin.'

Lis Munson smiled encouragement and all was well.

Our own performances took up the last week of the festival; the week preceding this, other schools and colleges of education brought entertainment to us. Travelling children's theatre groups were also invited. The most enthralling of these was Ed Berman's anarchistic company from outer space, who deserve to be savoured much more than the Arts Council allows for. Student teachers who had visited the school were also invited back to do something for us. They usually did come back, in spite of the fact that it meant working through their vacation for many of them. The last day was set apart for our Christmas parties and this was giving us a problem – a straightforward matter of finance. The school had been drained and another fund-raising spree would have finished us all off, there were sweets to buy and we had nothing left to barter with. A letter arrived; one glance at the heading – HM Prison, Pentonville – assured it of an immediate scrutiny, and any latent fears were quickly dispelled. The prisoners had collected money throughout the year and were offering us an enormous hamper of sweets, purchased out of their prison wages. The Governor in his letter had asked when I would like the goods delivered. We talked about it in the staffroom and one of the teachers, I think it was Molly, said over her coffee –

'One of those guys, one of the prisoners I mean, should be our Santa Claus this year.'

There was immediate support for the idea. If he were covered in a beard and all the red and fur paraphernalia, we would not have to worry about identity and it would be a good day out for him. In distributing the sweets, he would be going in for more than just an exercise in social rehabilitation.

The Governor had arranged the situation carefully and well.

He told me that it was his last term of office and remarked that this occasion was one of his most pleasant tasks preceding his pending retirement. It was easy to pick out which of the eight men was our Santa Claus, although all were in civilian clothes. He was very pale and drawn and looked as though he had spent part of his life in a darkened mushroom patch. I was short of sherry glasses: this was fortunate, as it gave me an opportunity of giving him a huge drink in a tumbler. I laughed when I gave it him and so did he and from then on I felt he would enjoy his new role. I don't know whether it was the sherry or his fresh seasonal identity, but the red and white and whiskered gentleman's complexion seemed to glow a little when he took up his sack of individually labelled parcels for delivery. The school was bursting with life and excitement. End-of-term class parties were in full swing in each room and the decorations and artwork everywhere were a conclusive testament to the success of our festival.

The infants gave back as much as they received. In exchange for chocolate, liquorice allsorts, and sherbert fizzes, they clapped him, sang for him and danced for him without any coercion. Once again, older children were not cynical about a visiting Santa Claus, they were under no illusions as to the disguise, but they accepted it all with goodwill and humour. This kind of adolescent reception is rare at the secondary stage, except perhaps in an all-age school. The older children did not want to destroy the sense of wonder or fun of the younger ones and went along with Santa Claus as part of a total effort. The older girls accepted their talcum powder with remarks like,

'Thanks a lot, hope you're not going to be too cold over Christmas. I'll think of you when I'm havin' a bath.'

When the last balloon had sagged or popped and the mountains of jelly and blancmange had been bulldozed away, our special visitor said his farewells. He took off his black cape and red smock, removed his whiskers and gaiters and was once again ready to be escorted away. I was sure he had enjoyed it all, yet it was difficult to know what to say to him.

'Well, goodbye – thank you for coming, we've never had such a convincing Santa Claus. I hope everything works out for you.'

He smiled and nodded, he didn't want to say anything and I accepted his nod and smile. There were no reindeer outside and the last I saw of him he was walking towards a large dark blue car escorted by four blue-and-grey-suited gentlemen.

Nothing is quite so void as a school without children in it. The empty building which is left must be the nearest thing to outer space that we have on earth. When the last remnants of our parties had been cleared away and the last child had returned to collect something he or she had forgotten, this is how it all seemed. Even the decorated hoops and clusters of balloons suspended from the hall ceiling appeared to say it was all over. Teachers and helpers had remained in the staff-room for a farewell Christmas drink. It was three days before Christmas and many of them had to repeat the festival once more in personal terms with regard to their own families. Two or three glasses of wine relaxed all of us, but looking around the staffroom the fatigue was evident in spite of the kinship and cordiality.

'All that exchanging of Christmas cards seems so pointless after all of this. I've made a list of people who I am sending cards to, and I suppose they are all doing just the same. When you think about it, the time and money involved, it seems to have lost all sense of proportion. Then there are presents to buy, it's a pity we can't just give when we want to. I wonder when all this kind of exchange and mart Christmas ordeal started?'

'Oh, come on Betty you're being stingy, you enjoy receiving cards don't you?'

'No she's not, she's right, we are all going to stuff ourselves

sick with food and go through family rituals that have nothing
to do with us. Look here, they are stopping bombing Vietnam
just for Christmas. We're just as bad, pretending to be nice
for a few days, then it's back to the everyday carnage.'

'Oh it's not as bad as all that, we've had a good time here
haven't we? Would you say all that we've done over Christmas has been a waste of time?'

'No, but don't you see, it's not real compared with what is
going on everywhere.'

'You can't say that, it means you'll give up doing what you
do and being what you are, that's as bad as dropping bombs.
That kind of defeatism spreads.'

The staff conversation drifted on from the serious to the
banal domestic. Maggie extended open invitations for people
to drop in at her place.

'I should warn you though, we are all off meat, in fact we
are all eating cauliflowers, my Pete (her son) has a theory
about it.'

'What else is there besides cauliflower?'

'That's it, just cauliflower. I might go all daring and give it
one or two different sauces from time to time, but we are
being really strong about it. Our blood will be absolutely pure
in two weeks, it's got it all in this book I've told you about.'

'I'll call and see you after the cauliflower-Christmas is over
Maggie.'

I made an attempt to thank them formally for all their hard
work but they laughed and joked my postured compliments
away. Postured or not they were meant, and gratitude for this
hard-working team I could never keep in short supply. It
wasn't necessary for me to offer this kind of pontificated
appreciation. One of the children, during the final end-of-term
assembly, put it much better than I had. The children were all
leaving the hall, shaking hands with the staff and exchanging
goodbyes. George Duford was a fourteen-year-old West Indian
referred as a school refusal/truant. He was never away from

school whilst he was with us. As the leave-takings were going on, he stood up and clapped his hands. All activities stopped and we looked in his direction. This was out of character for him. He clapped his hands again and I realised that his stammer was holding up what he had got to say. We waited . . .

'Th-, th-, th-, th-, th-, damn!' The words just wouldn't come out for him. Then they came, in a deep voice which swept through the hall. 'Three boos for the holidays,' he shouted. Coming from a boy who had adamantly refused to attend school for much of his life, this was as good a testimonial as any of us could have hoped for.